'This is a book that every man needs to read! Wagner has a way of making practical, no-bullshit, life-changing wisdom totally accessible.'

Dominic Carubba, men's coach, author of *7 Pages to Success*

'Such an important and accessible read for men of today. David's compelling voice offers men the most perfect distinctions – and the best questions – to be both powerful AND happy.'

Elena Brower, yoga teacher and author of *Art of Attention*

'David Wagner is a transformational teacher, dedicated leader, and dear friend. David is on a committed path of service, guiding others to awaken to their inner wisdom and authentic power. I am proud to call David a dear friend and spiritual running buddy.'

Gabrielle Bernstein, *New York Times* bestselling author of *Miracles Now*

'There is only one path to enlightenment: One must walk through the fire of their own pain. As men, we are tempered by that fire into the walking embodiment of not only strength, but compassion for others, adaptability to life, and vital passion for living. David was born to be a leader of men; he has walked through the fire; he shows men the way.'

Marcus Ambrester, author of *Pillars of Awesome Relationships*

'*Backbone* is a fabulous title – and is exactly what David has given me – a spiritual backbone with which I can blast off and accomplish my goals and live my dreams – bravo!!!'

Lev Gorn, actor on *The Americans* (FX Network)

'David's work with men comes at a critical time in our culture. He is facilitating the growth and evolution of the modern man in a way that is compassionate, impactful, and easy to connect with. A born story teller, David will deepen your understanding of what it means to be a man and live a compelling and fulfilled life. He is a man of deep integrity, honesty, and humor.'

John O'Connor, men's group leader and executive coach

'David Wagner's spiritual work with men has helped countless men to have better lives. In a world that controls language toward neutrality, and weakens traditional gender lines, where men are shamed for "acting like a man," David gets straight to the point of what it means to be a spiritual man, and to reach a deeper level of understanding of what it means to be a man. Man, *Backbone* is a good read that has long lasting spiritual resonance.'

Ron Silver, restauranteur-chef and author of
Bubby's Brunch Cookbook

'For decades we have waited for a book that specifically addresses the challenges that modern men face. So many of the self-help books on the market have a feminine edge and do not speak directly to a man's masculinity. The message men have been given so far is that they have to get in touch with their feminine side if they want to embrace change. This book blows that out of the water and is a total paradigm shifter. It enables men to fiercely transform, working with their masculinity instead of against it. Men all over the world will be saying: "Finally a book that actually speaks to me in my language." This book is the go-to men's book of this decade, and is a total game changer for men from all walks of life.'

Sasha Allenby, author of *Matrix Re-imprinting Using EFT*
and CEO of Wisdompreneurs Publishing

BACKBONE

THE MODERN MAN'S ULTIMATE GUIDE TO PURPOSE, PASSION, AND POWER

DAVID H WAGNER

WATKINS

Sharing Wisdom Since
1893

Malo periculosam, libertatem quam quietam servitutem.

I prefer dangerous freedom to peaceful slavery.

Thomas Jefferson

This edition published in the UK and USA 2015 by
Watkins, an imprint of Watkins Media Limited
19 Cecil Court
London WC2N 4EZ

enquiries@watkinspublishing.co.uk

Design and typography copyright © Watkins Media Limited 2015
Text Copyright © David Wagner 2015

David Wagner has asserted his right under the Copyright, Designs
and Patents Act 1988 to be identified as the author of this work.

1 3 5 7 9 10 8 6 4 2

Typeset by JCS Publishing Services Ltd, www.jcs-publishing.co.uk

Printed and bound in the United States of America

A CIP record for this book is available from the British Library

ISBN: 978-1-78028-828-4

www.watkinspublishing.com

CONTENTS

INTRODUCTION

Over the past several decades there's been a 'self-help revolution,' but men have not been included in it. It's not that we've been excluded, it's just that, by and large, we've opted out. The women in our lives have gone into therapy and yoga, and have bought the relationship and spirituality books. But we, for the most part, have left the personal-transformation stuff up to them. Some of us in desperate situations have gone into therapy. Some of us have even made it to the yoga rooms and self-help retreats. But most of us have stayed at home. When we have been adventurous, or when we've been dragged to the yoga or meditation class or personal-development workshops, we found ourselves outnumbered, surrounded by women. Up until now, the self-help, New Age, personal-transformation world has been a feminine realm.

It's not that we don't need help. These days many men are suffering a kind of quiet, desperate, lost-ness. As a group, we're not doing so well on an inner level. We may be able to make decent money, take care of our responsibilities, stay out of trouble, and keep the appearance of holding it together. But, on the whole, most of us aren't happy. Or at least you could say we're not deeply happy. Too many men today would say that they don't feel truly powerful or truly free – at least not as powerful and free as they'd like to be.

Even if men are powerful professionally, too often they are impotent in other areas. Many men don't know how to stand up for themselves in relationships. We're not sure how to deal with our dark emotions or our sexuality. Most of us can't relate deeply with other men. We don't know what's really important to us. We lack deep purpose. We lack passion. As a group, we don't have depth and power. In short, we lack backbone. And without backbone, we have a hard time making our way in this ever-demanding, ever-changing world.

If you are like the many men I have worked with, this may be speaking to you on some level. Before we move on, I want to ask some questions so you can start to look at this for yourself right here from the get-go. Be honest in your answers.

- How happy are you?
- How satisfied are you with your life?
- On a scale of 1 to 10, how would you rate your relationships?
- What about your work life or career?
- How is your physical health?
- What about your spirituality?
- Do you find that you're growing as a man, as a human being? Or are you stagnant? Is there a part of you that senses that there's more to life, more to being alive, than you're currently experiencing?

Introduction

If this little exam shows you that there's some room for improvement, you're not alone. Human life is a funny thing: it can be great or terrible, depending on how we do it. Few of us are able just to 'wing it' and really get the very most out of life. Most men need to do some adjusting, some self-work. We need training. This book is going to get you moving on that training path. It is designed to open a conversation that you have with yourself and the other men in your life – a conversation that's going to change the way you relate and contribute to your world.

The ideas that I'm sharing in this book come from my own journey as a man, my own journey of finding my backbone and learning how to live with it at the center of my life. My intention is to help you become your version of a deeply happy, powerful man – not my version or anyone else's version. I had to learn many of these lessons the hard way and I have watched countless other men try to slog through the shit without having this kind of guide. My aim is to help all men so that we can embrace our lives, celebrate our manhood, and revel in the best parts of a man's life. Being a man can be an awesome thing.

The Maori people of New Zealand have a great word: mana. Mana refers to the core potency of a man. It is his prestige, authority, self-control, power, influence, status, spiritual mojo, charisma, freedom, and ability to handle his life in a powerful way. We don't have a word like this in the Western world. But this is what we are after.

What does it mean to be a deeply happy, powerful man? Few men today even ask themselves that question. Because they don't want to ask that question, they wind up settling for just being a 'guy' – the half-baked, two-dimensional version of a man. It's easy to be a guy. All you have to do is be male and reach adulthood. There's no initiation, there's no training required. You're just a guy – and not much is expected of you. Stay out of trouble. Don't be a dick. Pay your bills.

If you want to graduate out of guydom and enter a powerful and happy man-hood, it takes some work. To be a fully alive, free-thinking, powerful man of vision takes honing, training, reflection, personal development, and a good dose of brutal hon-

> A man with backbone is fearless, robust, loving, wise, steady, fun-loving, and ready to protect and serve the world in which he lives.

esty. That's what we're going to do with you as you go through this book. There's a deeply happy, powerful man and a mediocre two-dimensional guy in each of us. We have to decide which one we want to invest in.

WHAT IS BACKBONE?

In this book we're going to look at what it means for you to have 'backbone.' When I say backbone, I'm speaking of a man's conscious masculine core strength. It's about knowing yourself deeply, about honing yourself, enhancing your core strengths and reducing your core weaknesses. It's about knowing where you want to go in your life and knowing how to be the man you need to be to get there. Every one of us has a backbone. It's not a matter of 'growing one' – it's about finding it. It's about deeply examining ourselves, investing in our core selves, and choosing the kind of man we want to be. This book is a guide to help you learn to be a deeply happy, truly powerful, purpose-driven, passionate man.

When a man has backbone he knows what he stands for and what he won't stand for. A man with backbone lives from a place of bigness instead of pettiness and smallness. A man with backbone has learned to master his masculine energies and take charge of his life. He knows who he is, he knows what he's here for, and he spends his time on his mission in life. A man with backbone is fearless, robust, loving, wise, steady, fun-loving, and ready to protect and serve the world in which he lives. A man with backbone fully enjoys all that life has to offer, while taking care of his world in a most excellent way – not because someone else gave him a high standard, or because he's in competition to be a winner, but because he is operating from a place where he knows what is true for him and he is living that truth.

BACKBONE AND THE MODERN MAN

In earlier times, there wasn't such a need for a book like this. Good fathers would teach their sons what it meant to be a man. The dads and other older men took it upon themselves to mentor the young men of their community and teach the boys what they needed to know about honor, power, sex, and the natural world. In those days, boys worked side by side with their dads and learned through observation what it was to be masculine. And it was crucial that men had strength: most men in the past were required to do hard physical labor. Most men were required to fight in combat, or at the very least have the skills and strength needed to fight, defend their property, or protect their families. In many cultures, boys weren't considered men in their society until they had proven themselves in some way.

In those days, men were known for their bravery and their dignity, and there was such a thing as masculine beauty. Men really cared what other men thought of them – especially older men. Those days are long gone. Our dads didn't teach us, our schools didn't teach us, our society won't teach us, and our women can't and really shouldn't teach us what it means to be a man. It's up to us. It won't happen automatically and we won't learn it by watching TV or playing video games.

Since the 1950s, women have been on a massive evolutionary curve as they've stepped up to assume more powerful positions in the world. Over these same decades, men, for the most part, have taken a step back so as not to obstruct this process. Women have been forced to empower themselves and develop in internal and external ways. But the many resources that evolved to help women grow and transform – the therapies and other kinds of 'heart work' – have done so in a way that is not particularly man-friendly.

This book is something much needed today – a masculine paradigm for transformational work. I want men – all kinds of men – to be able to go deep, know themselves, heal themselves, transform themselves, without sacrificing their sense of manhood. In fact, with this work, we are entering the transformational arena *through our manhood*. It's time for men to step up and catch up – and to do it in our own way.

The work we're doing helps everyone, not just men. We aren't suggesting that men once again become the dominant gender in society. Living with backbone isn't about becoming a macho jerk. It's about a man empowering himself to rise up without anyone else having to shrink down. A man with backbone is able to partner with a powerful woman – if he so chooses – and help her to be even stronger. Our vision is a vision where everyone rises.

It's not about just giving you 'something else to do.' Men have enough to do. Nor is it something else to measure yourself by and come up feeling short. We have too many voices – inner and outer – telling us that we need to do more and be more. This is about you making the most of your life as a man. It's going to benefit your whole world, but ultimately, it's for you.

In this book we're going to look at ourselves deeply. We're going to learn what we stand for, and what we fall for. We'll look at how we live and how we think. We'll look at our habits, our wiring, our conditioning, and we'll learn ways to undo the old conditioning, and rewire ourselves in better, more powerful ways. For some of us, it's a massive overhaul that needs to happen. For others, this work will just be a tune-up. Whatever you do, whoever you are, and however you relate to all this stuff, this book will give you the tools to make the transformation to be more of the man you want to be.

This book won't necessarily get you laid more, or make you rich. It won't teach you how to pick up women, or boost your testosterone, or help you get a promotion. What it will do is help you to define what it means to you to be a deeply happy, truly powerful man who knows how to get the very best of everything *from* life and also give the very best of himself *to* life.

MY BACKBONE

As I said earlier, I had to learn a lot of this stuff the hard way. I was born in the American Midwest in the 1970s. I was one of four rambunctious sons of a mild-mannered, functioning-alcoholic dad, and an unhappy, alcoholic, dominating mother. Dad never taught us much about being boys or men. We were left to figure it out ourselves. We learned what we learned from older boys, from TV, from *Penthouse* magazine. All of us got into drinking and drugs pretty young. Fortunately, I was the worst with the drugs and alcohol. I say fortunately as I took a hard fall and ended up getting sober when I was just 16. I've been sober ever since.

Getting sober way back then was the catalyst for me to start on a path of conscious living. I really had no other choice. And I loved it. I mean, it wasn't 'cool' or 'fun,' but I found that I loved to work on myself. Once I got over my initial resistance, I started to enjoy going to AA meetings and talking about my inner life. I liked helping others who were trying to get clean. AA introduced me to prayer and meditation and, once I made it my own, I found I liked the spiritual stuff and was good at it.

I never had much interest in school, studying art for a while, then psychology. When I found good teachers and deep teachings, I went whole hog into personal-transformation work, and found myself on a path of hardcore Eastern spiritual training. Instead of going to grad school, I went to India. I spent my twenties living more or less like a monk: living in ashrams (spiritual centers), gaining some much-needed discipline, practicing celibacy, learning about service, the Indian wisdom teachings, and mastering my meditation practice. I found many substitute dads in my teachers and mentors there. They were the senior monks and spiritual scholars who had woven their lives around what they found most important. They taught me that.

But looking back now at the 'spiritual guy' that I was, I see how – even though I had a deep understanding of the Eastern teachings, and a high level of mastery of the mystical practices – I was still 'unbaked' as a man. I didn't know how to deal with money or women. I had very few male friends, and very little idea about my deep passions in life. When I was about 30, I married a nice girl from the ashram. I did everything I was 'supposed' to do, but really I was playing a role.

All of this came crashing down when fate rolled in and I blew up my life. In 2007 I went through a massive spiritual awakening experience that unlocked my consciousness on a deep inner level and allowed me to see and feel that I wanted more from life. After that experience, I became uncaged in a certain way – but I didn't yet have the man-training or honor code that I needed to 'run free' in a responsible way. I fell in love and started having sex with one of my female students, an amazing woman who later became the mother of my children. I split from my wife in a very painful divorce. I lost my home, most of my friends, and severely shook up the little community of students who had gathered around me in those days.

Introduction

That blow-up hurt a lot of people and it was more personally painful than anything I had ever experienced. But I consider that passage to be one of the holiest, most transformational times in my life. What I was learning wasn't about Spirit, or yoga, or something esoteric. I was learning about me. I was learning about life. I was learning about being a man. It was during this time that 'men's work' became the obvious thing I needed to focus on for my personal development. I had read *Iron John* in college some 15 years before. I was part of a men's group then, and read many of the 'men's movement' books that were coming out in those days. It wasn't until that gut-wrenching time of transition and grief in my late thirties that it all made sense.

Because of the nature of the blow-up, I didn't have a lot of female shoulders to cry on, and so I started to reach out to my network of men. My men – teachers like Gabriel Halpern, and friends like men's coach Dominic Carruba – were there for me. They answered my calls in the middle of the night, they hugged me and let me cry, and they kicked my ass and spoke to me with brutal honesty. They made me laugh, told me their stories, and pulled me through the mud to the other side. Some of my other close male friends fell away – men who weren't able to show up and be with me during that time. I learned how much it could hurt to have a 'brother' leave you hanging in a moment of real need.

I dug out *Iron John*, and re-read books like Moore and Gillette's *King Warrior Lover Magician*, and went into a deep dive, digging down into me, my manhood and my bullshit, to find my hunger for a passion-filled, robust, masculine life.

My teaching changed. I started focusing less on meditation and cultivating peace and serenity, and more on no-bullshit life transformation. I started working with more men, and my life's vision started to take shape, but it wasn't until 2011 that the whole thing erupted into fullness for me. In August 2011, I was leading a retreat in India when I got a call from Taryn (my former-student-turned-life-partner). She was pregnant with our first child, and had to undergo some kind of genetic testing for the baby while I was away. I was nervous and concerned about her wellbeing and the outcome of the test, but nothing could prepare me for what she said over that crackling Indian cellphone line:

'Your son is fine.'

Up until then, we didn't know the gender of the baby, and had both assumed it was a girl.

There was silence, then: 'We're having a son.'

In the movies, men are always very happy to hear that their child is a boy. It wasn't like that for me. Hearing the news that our baby was a boy was a like a kick in the stomach. A *son*. In my mind, a girl was easy. I knew women, and I had several nieces and god-daughters. But the idea of being a dad for a son suddenly brought a huge rush of unresolved feelings about my father and a whole host of other heavy emotions to the surface. Having a son meant that I had to be the father to a boy, and teach someone else how to be a man. I knew how hard things can be between fathers and sons and the prospect of me being that father which a son has issues with completely freaked me out.

Looking back, I can see now that in that moment I got a vocation, a sacred calling. In that heavy kick in the gut, I felt Spirit speaking to me. I felt the universe pushing me with two huge masculine arms into the next phase of my teaching and my mission in life. I needed to get my 'man shit' together ASAP. Not just for me, and not just for my son, but because the men of our world need help. Our modern world is not an easy place for boys and men. In that moment I heard the man-angels sing to me and then push me toward this moment, writing this book for you.

When I got back from India, I again redoubled my efforts, studying what was out there for men, and going deeper into my own journey. I started a men's group in my home city and began doing transformational workshops and retreats just for men. I haven't looked back. This work is changing the game for men. It's saving marriages and saving lives and helping all kinds of men get their shit together and get happy and free.

I love doing this work because of what I get to learn in the process. I can sit in a meditation workshop as a meditation master, or a master facilitator, but I can never sit in the front of a group of men as a 'master man' or a 'master father.' I've learned a great deal and have improved my game as a man in many ways, but it is the ultimate work in progress. I am right in this whole beautiful mess with you.

HOW TO USE THIS BOOK

Backbone is not meant to be a book of ideas, it's meant to be a guidebook. It's like a course in book form. I'm not going to tell you what it means to be a better man, but I am going to guide you through the questions and examinations that will help you figure out what that means for you. The book is somewhat systematic, like one of my intensive courses or training programs. Every section has some ideas and material as well as questions for reflection and exercises to take the material deeper.

You figure out what works best for you. You may choose to 'do the book' like a course, working through each section before moving on. Or you might want to read all the way through now and then go back to do the exercises. The key point to make this work for you is to take it personally. In other words, have the awareness that everything you read here is about you. The examples I give and the case studies I describe may not be *exactly* like you, but they are for you and for your transformation.

The Exercises

As a teacher, I find that people learn much better if they are engaged with content – rather than just having it rammed down their throats. In my workshops and courses, I always teach in a highly interactive, conversational way. In that same style, I have included sections called 'Brutal Honesty' with exercises and questions throughout the book. Don't skip these exercises. Over the years I've noticed that men don't like to be told what to do. They resist doing the exercises in courses and retreats. They don't like to raise their hand and share in front of the group. Man – just do it! It's for you.

Of course you can do it at your own pace. You might want to read *Backbone* all the way through once, and then go back through and do the exercises and questions later. The exercises are what will make this truly real for you and help you actually do the work and get the results.

I know this is a stretch for some of you. I'm going to ask you to be brutally honest with yourself. In my experience Brutal Honesty is one of the best medicines for men on a path of transformation. Brutal Honesty doesn't always have to be brutal. You may see some unsavory things about yourself – but you'll see some beautiful powerful aspects too.

Throughout the book, I'm going to ask you to do some Journaling – capturing your ideas in writing. I've been doing this for years and find it to be an essential practice. Your journal can be handwritten, or a special private file on a computer or device. The important thing is that it is private. Your journal becomes one place where you can say anything, express anything, ask any question, rant, bitch, moan, and complain. Of course you can also write your wisdom and express gratitude and prayers there too. I take a journal wherever I go. I use it for strategy, for a dumping ground, for a container of my highest and lowest and goofiest ideas.

When it's time to do the exercises, take a moment to get quiet within yourself. You might even want to close your eyes and center your attention on your breath for a few rounds. Then open your eyes, read the questions, and capture what's true for you.

Group Work

If possible, get a second copy of the book for a buddy and go through the process of reading the book together. This kind of partnered work isn't for every man, but it's good to be able to discuss this stuff with someone. If you're already in a men's group, you can even use *Backbone* as input for your group conversation.

Inner Work

The other practice that makes the material here really sink in is to do some quiet contemplation after you've read a passage. When you finish a session of reading, take a moment to reflect on what hit you, what stirred shit up for you, turned you on, or pissed you off. I've included exercises and questions for you throughout the book, but you need to stay alert to notice what pushed your buttons or got you thinking. My students know me as a first-class shit-stirrer. I am not an inspirational speaker. I am a transformational teacher. It's easy to inspire someone. It's a whole other thing to guide them through a lasting transformation. Training sessions with me are not usually cuddly, nicey-nice sessions of positive affirmations. I challenge people. I challenge assumptions and will call you out if I sense you're selling yourself short or bullshitting me or playing small. I can only reach so far through these book pages, so it's up to you to get in there and see what the material riles for you. One of the men that mentored me in my early days of sobriety was a sober man named Lonny. Lonny

worked at a cemetery digging graves. He used to say 'the deeper
you dig, the deeper you get.' So dig. Get a journal, use it to write
your reflections and questions. Use it to capture your vision for
your life and your notes along the way. Use it to help you dig in
deep. The bottom line is, it's ultimately up to you.

Introspection

This might be obvious to you, but just in case it isn't, the path we're
outlining in this book requires introspection. In other words, looking
within. It requires us to look inward and look deeply at ourselves.
This is a new thing for many men. For the most part, men aren't
taught to introspect. We're taught to look outward and get stuff
done. We're taught to keep moving and not overcomplicate things
by reflecting on them too much. If life makes us happy, we're happy.
If life is too hard, we're unhappy. If something is off in our life or in
our world, we're taught to find out who or what is to blame. Rarely
are we taught to look deeply in the mirror. Rarely are we taught to
examine our deep motives, fears, dreams, and inner blockages.

This point is so simple, it's easy to miss. Your mind, your
thoughts, your feelings, your attitudes, your beliefs, and your
assumptions all have a huge impact on your experience of life. We
walk through life looking through the lens of our 'outlook.' The
quality, health, and clarity of that outlook make a huge difference
to our life experience. If there is something warped in our outlook,
the world looks warped. If we see the world through a negative
attitude – also known as 'wearing our shit goggles' – everything
looks like shit. When we live our life in a tired, depleted state of
mind, everything feels really hard. When we have the courage to
look inward and change what's happening in our hearts and heads,
we change everything.

Part One
THE JOURNEY

THE RED ROAD AND THE THREE KEYS

In this first section, I want to lay out the basic idea of finding what it means to be a conscious man. It's easy to say that we need to be strong, get happy, and live our vision. But what does that actually mean? Religious men or men who belong to traditional societies have it a lot easier than we do as modern men. They have pretty clear guidelines to follow, and clear definitions of concepts like honor, manhood, and potency. Their cultural framework tells them what the 'good life' is supposed to look like. All they need to do is color inside the lines and conform to their society's idea of a man and they're all good. (They're probably not all good.)

The point is, few among us today have such clear lines to color within. We have to find our own way to be and our own definitions of the good life. It's one thing for me to share what backbone means for me in my life. For you, it might be similar, but it might also be very different. This section is going to help you look at yourself and see where you're at and what having backbone means for *you*.

1

THE RED ROAD

The Lakota tradition describes two roads or paths that every man must choose between: the Red Road and the Black Road. The Red Road is the road of honor, wisdom, power, and vision. The Black Road is the road of pettiness, dishonor, selfishness, and unconsciousness. The Red Road is described as narrow, winding, and difficult to follow. You have to be alert and watch every step. The Black Road, on the other hand, is described as wide, easy-to-follow, and very popular. You can sleepwalk down the Black Road, and there is always plenty of company there. To walk the Red Road, you have to stay awake. The path is always changing and often challenging. When we walk the Red Road, we become stronger, wiser, and better with time. When we walk the Black Road, we just get old and stupid.

I like this idea of the two roads as a metaphor for how we want to live as men. Do we choose to be conscious, growing, working on ourselves, and taking on life as an adventure? Or do we choose to just drift along in life and be the victim of our bad habits and unconscious ways of being? Do we choose just to go with the herd of half-alive, half-happy, half-awake people, staring at the screens of our TV or computer, getting older and weaker year by year? Or do we choose to walk the less popular road of

> When we walk the Red Road, we become stronger, wiser, and better with time. When we walk the Black Road, we just get old and stupid.

wakefulness and become a student of life, a carrier of wisdom, and servant of goodness in this world? It's up to us.

This book is laying out a Red Road path to help move us toward being fully empowered men of vision who know who we are and know what we're here for. This process is what I call finding your backbone.

THE MIDLIFE AWAKENING

We all know about the 'midlife crisis' many men go through. They hit 40 and start wearing hip clothes or they get a sports car or a young girlfriend. They seem to freak out and appear to be chasing their youth. That's not my experience as a man in my forties and as someone who works with men. It's more like this: Most men don't really know themselves very well, especially when they're young. We marry the wrong person, we suppress our passions so we can live the life we think we're supposed to live. But we signed up for that life based on bad information. We didn't deeply know ourselves. In this way, men wade forward into their marriages and careers 'for better, for worse' and gradually get more and more entrenched in their lives. Some men get into their thirties or forties and then something happens. They start to feel the pressure of time; they start to get a sense of their mortality. They sense their limited life span and 'go for it.' But, again, they often go for it based on bad information. Instead of doing the work to know themselves and create a new life of vision, the midlife-crisis guys do the obvious things: get laid, buy toys, have more fun. This kind of midlife freak-out has short-lived benefits and often long-term consequences.

What I'm doing here is giving men a chance to have an awakening. It may happen at midlife or at the end of life or in your twenties. Every man is different. Most of us become ripe for this self-work in our mid-thirties. Sometime in our teens most of us will have come up with an idea of 'what kind of man we are.' Then we go live that version of life. Most of us run out of script around 35. This is when the midlife crisis starts to brew. This book sets out to give us a chance to pre-empt a midlife freak-out by digging in and getting to know ourselves – setting out on a Red Road of vision and purpose and passion and clarity.

THE WILDMAN

One of the pioneers of the men's work that happened in the 1980s and 1990s was the great Robert Bly. In his book *Iron John*, Bly uses the archetype of the 'Wildman' to describe the essential energy that lives within every man. He called this energy our 'deep masculine.' From this point of view, the work we're doing here is not so much about making ourselves something better, or making ourselves something that we're not. It's about reclaiming something essential about ourselves that has been lost. If a man chooses the Red Road, he must come to terms with this deep masculine energy and own his inner Wildman.

Samuel Johnson wrote, 'He who makes a beast of himself gets rid of the pain of being a man.' The word 'beast' has become a negative thing, but I don't see it like that. In the purest sense, a beast is a beautiful thing. It is a creature living its true nature. This is what is meant by wild when we say Wildman. We're not talking about a hell-raiser or a party animal, or a man who goes berserk. The Wildman is that part of us that that is still a beast, like a plant or animal living in its natural, wild, untamed state. It's a wild thing, deeply intelligent, strong, and instinctual. Think of your favorite wild animal moving and living in its natural habitat. It isn't berserk: it is beautiful and powerful and miraculous in a natural sort of way. Wild beasts – even the most ferocious ones – have a sort of grace about them. Most of us as men have lost that wild grace. In our domesticated lives we've become awkward, unintelligent, and flabby – figuratively and literally.

As we become awake and find our backbones as men, we become beasts again in the most beautiful sense of the word. We take back some of what we've lost. We discover or uncover our Wildman; we honor him and give him some air to breathe. That inner Wildman is there with us at work, in our relationships, choosing our food, enjoying our life.

A man in possession of this Wildman energy is like a beast: self-possessed, wild, and therefore free. He's not owned by anyone or anything on the outside, and he's also not held back by his fears or insecurities from the inside. He isn't a slave to his addictions or chained up by his petty desires. Just as the beast is driven by its role in its ecosystem and its natural duty – whatever that is – a deeply happy, powerful man is driven by his vision for his life and lives according to his code of honor.

Unlike a moose or raccoon that has a very simple and limited mission in life, a man is a complex creature with many complex needs and facets. Unlike the wolves or red-tailed hawks that have their duty in life pretty well spelled out for them, a man has to find his own way in life. We have to discover what our duty is, what our gift is, what our vision is – and live it. This is, I believe, our nature. Just as it's the nature of a fish to swim, eat, breed, and die, so it is our nature to learn, know ourselves, love, create, and serve.

When we lack backbone, when we haven't done the work to know ourselves, when we're caught in our inner bullshit and living from a Black Road mediocre place, we aren't giving our gifts, we're not really growing. We aren't living up to our nature. Our inner Wildman is stuck in a box, trapped beneath a civilized mask.

THE OLD MAN

Old men in our modern Western world don't get much respect. When most Westerners think of a grandfather, we think of a cute old guy that we love and humor, but we don't take him too seriously. In every traditional society, elders are not only treated with respect, they are revered as living treasures of wisdom. I want to rekindle the culture of the wise old man, the true elder. In traditional Maori society, it is said that if a man has mana, that mana just gets stronger and stronger as he ages. Even as their physical power decreases, their inner mojo just gets stronger. If we find our backbone now and walk our Red Road from now on, we can look forward to being not just older when we get old, but better, deeper, wiser, more powerful. Old men with real backbone are badasses.

THE WHOLE MAN

In the Lakota language there is a great word: wica (pronouced wichha), which means 'complete man.' It is a word that is distinct from wichasa which simply means 'man.' The word wica is used to distinguish great men, like the great Ogala leader Crazy Horse. A wica or complete man is a man who is virtuous and wise on the inside, but also a man who takes care of his business and acts with fearlessness and kindness and honor in his life. The wica were great men, men who found their place in legend and are celebrated in the Lakota oral tradition. I like this as a vision for what we're shooting for. Not just being ordinary men, but great men – complete men.

As we walk this Red Road, we gain access to all the different parts of ourselves: our bodies, our minds, our emotions, our spiritual intelligence, our grit, our creativity, our humanity, and our passion. We're no longer confined to the shallow cartoon of a guy like Homer Simpson. We are whole. We have dimensions, layers of depth.

We have a desire to serve and protect others, and we display an innate sense of leadership. Ideally, along with all this we have a sense of humor that helps us not take ourselves too seriously. And we should also have a sense of purpose and mission in life that make us take our life, our time, and our energy very seriously.

When we live with backbone, we are in touch with an innate sense of freedom, but at the same time, like a wild animal, we live in harmony with the world around us. The Whole Man has the ability to see the big picture, the whole picture. The Whole Man lives with a deep sense of interconnectedness. Our power, our bigness, is not solitary. It is part of a web of life. Our strength becomes our family's strength. Our wisdom becomes the wisdom of our community. There's a symbiosis. We know how to have the very best experience of life and also give our very best self to life. When we are in our power, we serve and uplift the people, places, and things around us. This is our natural state. We are contributors. People feel safe in our shelter. They feel protected.

When we have our backbone we are not afraid of challenges. We don't always choose the easy way of doing things. When we are in our power, we are BIG. No matter what size we are physically, we live with a sense of bigness. We have a big heart and big capacity for life. When you are walking your Red Road, you are a natural leader, a fierce warrior, a tender lover, and a wise mystic, all wrapped up into one.

THE DARK SIDE

No one is perfect. No life and no man are without their share of darkness. The Red Road is still a path through real life; it is not a rosy path. Men with backbone, men who have learned to own and operate their whole self, know how to handle the shadow side of life and the shadow side of themselves.

On the Red Road, we accept our failures and losses, and learn how to shoulder feelings like grief and shame and embarrassment. No man gets to 40 without some significant failures on his track record. And the real-life projects we get into such as marriage, fatherhood, business, and spirituality are impossible to do in a flawless way. The Red Road is a path where we are constantly learning by trial and error. We learn how to fall forward, get up, and keep moving. When we have our backbone intact, we aren't crushed by our failures, and we don't have to live in denial about them either. We learn how to deal with our failures and upsets and convert them into wisdom, healthy toughness, and humility. We learn how to be open about our stumbling and how to gain support from other men who are walking (and stumbling) along their own Red Roads. But we keep walking forward. That's the point.

Walking the Red Road means learning how to manage not only the failures and imperfections of life, but also the dark sides and imperfections of ourselves. We learn what our inner strengths and weaknesses are. We learn how to manage our weaknesses.

Sometimes this means eliminating the weaknesses, but sometimes that's not possible. Sometimes, a man with backbone must simply learn to keep his darkness in check – 'keep the Devil in the hole,' so to speak. You'll learn more about that in the chapter about getting free from your bullshit. For now, let's just say that if you're going to walk the Red Road, you need to know how to master your own dark side.

THE BLACK ROAD

You can't really say that a man 'chooses' the Black Road. The Black Road is just the default setting if a man doesn't choose to wake up, find his backbone, and take charge of himself. Some men from good families with good upbringing and conditioning are lucky: they walk a pretty happy Black Road. They just follow along in whatever way they're programmed to and do okay in life. But, for most of us, the Black Road is the road to pain, mediocrity, and an unfulfilling, dismal life.

A man on the Black Road 'is who he is.' He doesn't really reflect much on who he is or why he is as he is. He's semi-conscious, half-awake. The Black Road man's life is uncreative and unoriginal. He blames others for his fate in life. He makes decisions based on what is obvious and easy, and less risky. The Black Road travels through a life of lazy bondage. If life on the Black Road is 'good to him,' the unconscious man will be more or less content and count his blessings. But if life blows storms in his way, he is ill-equipped to handle them. He lacks ingenuity. He doesn't have the kind of wakeful intelligence that a man needs to navigate the problems of life. A man on the Black Road just trudges on and does his best to entertain himself and enjoy himself on the weekend. He lives with a sense of being slowly crushed by his life. His life is a weight that he's just strong enough to hold, but he's not strong enough to lift it high or really move it. Life just is. The Black Road's motto seems to be: 'Life's a bitch – and then you die.'

When we ask the question, 'Are you on the Red Road or the Black Road?' it's not really an either/or situation. The truth is, we have both of these options open to us every minute. Men who walk mostly on the Black Road surely have moments of greatness on their journey, and Red Road walkers often lose their way for a time. It's a journey; it's a process. We are constantly course-correcting and refining our life. We are always growing and changing and trying to invest in the best part of ourselves.

SUMMING IT UP

The Red Road – this is the road of honor, wisdom, power, and vision.

The Midlife Awakening – instead of getting lost in your midlife crisis, this book gives you the opportunity to make your midlife a time of self-discovery and tremendous growth.

The Whole Man – as we walk the Red Road, we gain access to all the different parts of ourselves: our bodies, our minds, our emotions, our spiritual intelligence, our grit, our creativity, our humanity, and our passion.

The Dark Side – we need to honor and own our shadow, our darkness. Not hide it, and also not use it as our guiding light. We need to know how to handle our dark side.

The Black Road – this is the default path of unconscious, unconsidered living. This is the path a man walks when he doesn't wake up, find his backbone, and take charge of himself.

BRUTAL HONESTY

Take an honest look at where you are in your life right now. Up until this point in your life, have you been mostly on a Red Road or a Black Road? How do you experience the difference? What do you feel when you consider shifting your approach to life and embracing a Red Road approach?

Take a moment to think about and write answers to the following questions:

- What are the areas of your life (money, work, relationships, etc.) where you find yourself mostly on the Black Road?
- What are the areas where you find yourself more on the Red Road?
- What improvements can you imagine in your experience of life if you were to take on this challenge and start living all the areas of your life with 'Red Road' awareness?

Use your journal to make some notes. Don't skip out on the journaling. When you put it in writing you're going to uncover some stuff about yourself that you won't discover just by thinking about it.

2

HAPPINESS AND POWER

If you ask them, most men would tell you that they would like to be powerful, free, and happy. Isn't it funny that so few really are? Growing up, we're taught that happiness is the result of having four basic elements in life: material wealth, vocational success, love, and good health. If you have these, you're happy. But we see again and again that it doesn't work that way. There are plenty of rich, successful, and healthy family men who are unhappy. We also see plenty of men who are sorely lacking in any of those four areas yet still manage to be really happy.

Here's the secret: Deep happiness doesn't come from having 'the big four.' Deep happiness is a whole other element. And like a career, a relationship, or a healthy body, our happiness needs special attention and nurture. There's a process of self-work and self-examination that men need to do to fully understand themselves and in order to tend to their basic happiness needs.

Most men these days aren't very good at this process. The kind of happiness we are talking about here is a contentedness that is our basic center of gravity in life, a happiness that's living deep in the marrow of our bones. This deep happiness – sometimes I call it radical happiness – is a hard-won, unconditional state of deep wellbeing that can't be shaken by the ups and downs of life. This deep happiness isn't a smiley-faced, cosy kind of glee that comes because some *thing* or some situation is the way you want it. This deep happiness comes because *your life* is the way you want it, and *you* as a man are the way you want to be.

It's the same with power. Strength, potency, mojo, power – these are core aspects of being a man. Every man wants to be strong. No man wants to be powerless or impotent. The kind of power we are thinking of here is not just a momentary state or a temporary position. We're not talking about winning anything or dominating anyone. The kind of potency we mean is a core state of being. True Power is the power that comes when you are steady in yourself and connected to your deepest true self. True Power is there for you when you know who you are, you have your demons in check and you're tapped into the ever-present living energy of the universe. It is unstoppable, unconditional, and doesn't rely on anyone or anything. This power is what we are at the core. It comes when we are rooted in our essence, our Soul Energy. This kind of core potency doesn't increase when we dominate others. In fact, it seems to thrive when everyone and everything – your family, your

> True Power is there for you when you know who you are, you have your demons in check and you're tapped into the ever-present living energy of the universe.

co-workers, your friends – are all thriving and powerful too. Having backbone means that you have core strength. The same way that your whole body is supported by your spine, your whole life of vision is supported by your mana – your backbone.

As we set out on the Red Road, we need to learn to make a basic shift: from outer focus to inner focus. We have seen again and again examples of outwardly focused men who have all the best things – all the success, all the love, and all the accolades from the world – but who are still miserable or alienated because they lack something on the inside. Think of the drug-addicted millionaire entertainers, or crash-and-burn celebrities in the tabloids. They're beautiful, talented, and rich, and everyone loves them, but they still aren't happy. Watch the news or read your history books to see the outwardly powerful men who become tyrants trying to satisfy the urge to overcome their inner feelings of impotence. Men with core power don't need to dominate others. Domination comes when inwardly impotent men have too much outer power. They have whole armies and nations under their control, but they can't control their own mind or know when to quit, or take care of their families.

On the other end of the spectrum from the fortunate-miserable people and the impotent tyrants, we know of men who have miserable outer circumstances, or who are totally stripped of outer power, but who still manage to be happy and powerful on an inner level. Think of Nelson Mandela in prison, or Viktor Frankl in Auschwitz.

Superficial power and momentary happiness are like empty calories. We can eat and eat and eat, but we're never full, and never nourished in a deep way. Also, like junk food, these empty-soul calories take their toll on us. Getting caught up in their pursuit is what brings on the Black Road conditions of hardness, passivity, or the naive chasing of bliss.

THE THREE KEYS TO HAPPINESS

I want to share with you something that was revealed to me. I call them the Three Keys to Happiness. If you truly learn these Three Keys, you will be well on your way to whatever transformation you're looking for. These Three Keys are the foundation of my whole approach to spiritual training and personal development. First, let me tell you the story of how they were revealed to me. This story can only be told in a men's book.

The Keys were revealed to me in 2012 when I was on a very special and sacred pilgrimage. The pilgrimage was to the Harley Davidson Motorcycle dealership in Great Neck, New York to buy my 2010 Harley Davidson FXDB Street Bob. People who know me know that I am an avid rider. Here in New York I'm known for rumbling up to my meditation class, ready to lead people into their peaceful, silent practice.

Earlier that year, my old motorcycle had been totally destroyed in 'Sandy,' the quasi-hurricane that ravaged this part of the country with floods. After several grueling weeks with nothing to ride, I finally got my insurance payment and was ready to get a replacement. I found the bike I was looking for, took the trip from Manhattan to Long Island, test rode the bike, loved it, and was in the process of finalizing the purchase when the Three Keys were magically revealed.

When you buy a motorcycle, there's a process. You can't just say, 'Yep – this one!' hop on, and ride away. First you have to haggle over the price, and then you have to arrange the financing, then the title, the insurance, etc. There's a process, and it takes a while. Remember, I had not been on two wheels in several weeks and was chomping at the bit to get on my new bike and ride it home. But I couldn't: I was stuck in an office at the dealership with a man filling out the paperwork.

I don't remember his name. He was a big man with long hair and a Harley T-shirt stretched over his big belly. Outside, the sun was going down, and I was getting impatient. The process seemed to be taking forever. Making small talk, the Harley guy asked, 'So, Dave, what do you do for a living?' I get asked this question all the time by people who really don't care. It's something people ask to break the silence. And what I do for a living is strange to a lot of people; it's not that easy to explain. I didn't really want to get into that whole conversation there. I wanted to get on my new bike and hit the road. So I gave a short, vague answer, trying to brush him off so he could focus on finishing the paperwork.

'I run a small business.'

'Oh, yeah? What kind of business?' He didn't look up from his papers. I didn't really think the Harley guy wanted to know about meditation, and the Red Road, and all the stuff I actually do in my business, so, again I tried to blow him off.

'It's a training business.'

'Oh, yeah? What kind of training do you do?' he asked. Now he had me up against a wall. I could have gone with one of my usual ordinary answers like 'Stress reduction' or 'Leadership,' but for some reason I said something much weirder:

'I train people to be happy.'

There was silence. Then the guy put his pen down on his desk, leaned back into his creaking chair, crossed his arms across his big belly and looked me in the face. 'Okay. So, tell me, Dave, what's the secret to happiness?'

He wasn't being an asshole, he was sincere. He was genuinely curious. If someone is for real, I don't care who they are or where we are – I'm happy to share my two cents with them. I really didn't want to blow him off. But the sun was setting and I didn't want to get into a long conversation. I wanted to get on the road! So, somehow Grace, or the Great Spirit, or the Old Gods smiled on me, and that's when it happened. Out of my mouth, I heard this:

'All of the deeply happy people that I know have two things in common: they know what their purpose in life is, and are on track with that purpose. And they have some kind of "spiritual connection" that works for them.'

A moment of silence passed, and my new friend thought about it for a second and then said, 'Yeah, I guess

The First Key gives us the power of fiery purpose, the Second Key connects us to the power of the universe, the Third Key gives us power because it gets us free from the stuff that holds us back and drains our energy.

that sounds about right.' He leaned forward, picked up his pen, and went back to his paperwork.

A few minutes later I got my new beautiful beast and was booming down the highway reflecting on that conversation. 'A clear purpose and a connection to Spirit. Is that it?' As I rode, I added a third important thing: People who are deeply happy, along with living their purpose and having a spiritual connection, also have, in one way or another, gotten free from the inner and outer bullshit that most unhappy people carry around. 'Wow, that's it!' I thought.

So the Three Keys are:
1   **Know your true purpose in life, and be on track with living your vision**
2   **Cultivate a strong and authentic spiritual connection**
3   **Get free from your bullshit**.

Each Key gives us tremendous power. The First Key gives us the power of fiery purpose, the Second Key connects us to the power of the universe, the Third Key gives us power because it gets us free from the stuff that holds us back and drains our energy. It took me 25 years of personal practice and a couple of decades of teaching others to realize it, but really the whole secret to deep transformation and success on the Red Road boils down to these Three Keys. These are the basic three mega steps that you'll need to take to really move into your life as a deeply happy, vision-driven, passionate, powerful man.

SUMMING IT UP

The Big Four – growing up, we have been taught that happiness comes from 'the big four': material wealth, vocational success, love, and good health.

Deep Happiness – this is a hard-won, unconditional state of deep wellbeing that can't be shaken by the ups and downs of life.

The Three Keys to Happiness

1   Know your true purpose in life, and be on track with living your vision.

2   Cultivate a strong and authentic spiritual connection.

3   Get free from your bullshit.

BRUTAL HONESTY

How have you have been searching for happiness in 'the big four' (material wealth, vocational success, love, and good health)? When you did experience happiness in one of these areas, what did you notice? Was it fleeting? Did you find yourself depending on it to 'make' you happy? Then what happened?

Now reflect on the Three Keys to Happiness. We are going to look at each one of these in detail in the next three chapters, but just on a first glance, how much of the following is true for you:

• I know what my purpose is and I'm on track with it.
• I have a strong, authentic spiritual connection.
• I deal with my bullshit.

Take a moment to journal your findings.

Now that we have raised the question of what it means to be deeply happy as a man, in the following chapters we'll get into each of the keys in more detail.

3

THE FIRST KEY

Without vision, people perish.

Proverbs 29:18

The First Key: Know your true purpose in life, and be on track with living your vision.

If you want to have backbone, you need to know what you're here for. It's the most essential thing for any man on the Red Road. Do whatever it takes to really know yourself and know your true purpose, your mission in life. This applies to everyone, but it is especially true for men. Our vision and our sense of purpose in life is our centerline, it's the foundation that we build a strong and wakeful life on. If we don't know our purpose or don't have a clear and potent vision for life, we are prone to be tormented, distracted, and depleted as we move through our existence. When we do know our purpose and live that purpose, our life is electrified, empowered, clearly directed, and deeply fulfilling.

When I say purpose and vision, I don't mean a mere goal or a 'life plan.' I mean our sense of what our life is for, and the overall way we envision our life and allow our purpose to manifest. It's the way we want our future to unfold. It's the way we want to live our life and how we imagine and 'see' ourselves living it. It's the way that we share our value, our gifts with our world. Our purpose and vision make up the honorable life path that we commit ourselves to walk.

The big difference between the Red Road and the Black Road for a man is this: A man on the Red Road lives with vision, he makes choices that are in alignment with his vision, and directs all of his life energies toward making that vision a reality. He chooses how he spends his time, how he earns and spends his money, the places where he lives, and the people he surrounds himself with. He chooses his life carefully and designs his life from a place of power and wisdom.

The man on the Black Road drifts through life like a stick in a stream. He makes his choices based on what he thinks he's supposed to do, or based on what is easiest. The Black Road is the path of least resistance. Sometimes it turns out okay, sometimes not. A man who wants to walk the Red Road does what he needs to do to identify his vision for life, and then does his damnedest to live according to it, constantly striving to be 'on purpose' and correcting himself when he's strayed off course. Often times, the way life is, we're far from perfect in this regard. What makes our road the Red Road is that we have a vision in the first place, and that we are committed to our vision in thought, feeling, word, and action.

When we have a sense of our deep purpose and we have a vision for our life, we have a destination, we have the directedness that is crucial for man to be happy and powerful. Later I refer to this as our inner King Power (see Chapter 8). When we have a vision and purpose, we have something that we can use to direct our life decisions. When we have a clear vision and purpose, we have the motivation we need to do the hard things that come our way and keep moving when we get pulled down or blocked in life.

I'm not talking about living for the future. I'm not talking about denying our happiness in the present moment for the sake of a 'someday goal.' When we live with vision, we live that vision in this moment, even when the whole vision hasn't come to fruition. The vision is either unfolding now or it isn't. We are either living from our power and wisdom, or we're living motivated by something else.

In order to have a vision for your life, you need to have a sense of your purpose.

PURPOSE

Men need to have a purpose in life. The more intense and clear their purpose, the more fuel they have to live their life and the more they can enjoy their core power. Men sometimes get freaked out when I am helping them to find their purpose. It can feel like a huge thing that you have to 'get right' in one attempt, or like some kind of divine mandate that descends on you from high above. Rarely does anyone simply wake up one day knowing their vision and purpose. Most men have found their purpose by doing intense and sincere seeking. Most men find their purpose through a combination of trial and error, persistence, and deep self-inquiry. No one is going to tell you what your purpose is. You have to uncover it. Often, you can just choose it. You can simply ask yourself, 'What do I want my purpose to be?' Sometimes it's as easy as that. Or sometimes it helps to ask, 'What was I born to do in this life?'

Backbone

Dharma and Swadharma

In the wisdom traditions of the East, there's a great word: *dharma*. There's no exact English translation of dharma. Dharma can mean duty, or righteousness. I like to think of it like the Chinese word *Tao* – which means 'the Way.' Dharma is the perfect natural order of things. Dharma can mean 'deep nature.'

For me, dharma is the force that makes the planets revolve around the Sun so perfectly. Dharma is what makes the plants grow and breezes blow. Dharma is the all-pervading natural force that keeps the universe in check and everything interacting perfectly in the natural world. It isn't all nicey-nice: lions eat antelopes, viruses wipe out populations, fire destroys forests, big fish eat little fish, and so on. There are darks and lights, easies and hards within dharma, but in the natural world it all works out and is in perfect balance. It is a kind of magnificent, rich harmony with every color and texture.

There's another Sanskrit word that's related to dharma: *swadharma*. Swadharma means 'one's own dharma.' A person's swadharma is the way that they, as an individual, fit into the greater universal dharma. Your swadharma is the natural role that you play in the wider universe. Everyone and everything has a swadharma. Nature makes the lion perfectly suited to live as a lion. A lion does only lion things, eats only lion food, breeds only with other lions. If any of this gets thwarted, the lion suffers, or it simply doesn't work. If a lion eats donkey food, he's not going to thrive. If he tries to breed with a zebra, it's just not going to work. In the same way, according to the Indian wisdom traditions, each man is also made to live his life in a certain way for a certain purpose. I love this teaching because it makes the whole 'finding your purpose' thing a lot more organic: we just have to follow what our deep nature is.

But here's the problem: The beasts – the lion, the plant, the fish – all have very set swadharmas. Animals and plants are born

38

or sprouted or hatched and just follow their natural life course perfectly. They know what to eat and where to live, who to mate with and how to hunt or produce fruit. Plants and animals don't even really seem to have a choice. We humans – or 'two-leggeds,' as the Native Americans call us – are different; we do have a choice. We have a mind, a deep psyche, and a special kind of soul that needs to find its dharma. Unlike the fox or the butterfly, we have the ability to lose track of our purpose and not know what we are.

We men have to find our purpose, our swadharma. When we do find it, and we start to live our purpose, we tap into that same kind of deeply connected strength that the lion, the pine tree, and the grizzly bear have. When we know who we are as men, and we know what our purpose is in life, we become very, very powerful. That's when we tap into that Wildman energy. We are living our Truth, our natural, powerful self. We have become wild in the best possible way. It's natural for a man to have backbone – all men have backbone – it's a matter of finding, investing in, and owning that backbone. I believe it's how nature intends us to be.

On the other hand, if we don't find our purpose, or deny our swadharma, or stay stuck in our addictions or disempowered life choices, like a lion living in a cage, we suffer. We fail to thrive. And if we don't know our purpose, if we don't follow our vision, we will likely be forced to follow someone else's vision. A man's energy is valuable. If we're not going to use our time and our life energies to follow our Truth, that energy is going to be gobbled up by the world. This rarely turns out well. There's a great verse in the *Bhagavad Gita* (3:35) that speaks about this:

Better to perform one's own dharma poorly than to perform another person's dharma well. Better is death in one's own dharma; living the dharma of another invites great peril.

Among all the people I've ever worked with in my career, this is the number one cause of unhappiness, depression, anxiety, and pain. When we try to live according to someone else's vision, it sucks. It sucks bad. It's like in earlier times, when gay men had to live totally straight lives with wives and children, putting on an act of being heterosexual, all the while feeling totally different inside. Don't think that gay men aren't the only men who keep their truth 'in a closet.' Most men hide their truth or avoid their truth to some extent. We might hide our Truth because we're trying to impress our father, or because we think we'd fail if we took a chance to live our dream. We live fake lives because we haven't done this work, we haven't taken the time to know who we really are. The path of living our Truth is the Red Road, it's the road less traveled.

It's not that we're fake or that we're putting on a conscious front. If we don't know what is true for us or if, for whatever reason, we don't accept what is true for us, we have no choice but to put on an act. We go through the motions that people expect us to go through. This is the ultimate expression of the Black Road man: plodding along through life like a slave, watching time go by, trying to keep himself entertained. Or, as one Indian master put it, 'committing suicide in installments.' It's not an exaggeration. Over the course of the phony half-lived life, we shrink, day by day, year by year. If you don't know what your purpose is you will end up becoming a slave to someone else's.

LIVING TRUE

One of the core mottos of the transformational work I teach is 'Love Hard – Live True.' We put it on T-shirts; one of our students even has it as a tattoo! I call it our battle cry. There's a tremendous amount of genuine power in a man who is 'living true.' Your family might not like or accept what is true about you, society might not like or accept what is true about you, and it might not be the most obvious way to make lots of money, but when you Live True, you align yourself

> If you don't know what your purpose is you will end up becoming a slave to someone else's.

with the same True Power that fuels the elephant, or the river, or the eagle. When you're connected to that deep natural force of dharma, little or nothing can stop you. Then you can 'Love Hard.' You live your life full-throttle and give your gift to the world completely.

Our goal as men walking the Red Road is to be fully alive and deeply directed. In the woods, you can tell the difference between dog tracks and the tracks of a wild dog – like a coyote, wolf, or fox: the domesticated dog tracks zig-zag and wander all over. The wild-dog tracks go in a straight line. A wild thing moves with purpose. Your path may be windy with many turns, but on this path you learn to keep walking forward, straight toward what is most important to you.

Get on Track

Let's look at that First Key again: 'Know your purpose in life, and be on track with living your vision.'

The second part of this key is super important. It's not enough just to know your purpose and have a vision for your life. To have this complete key, you need to also be on track with your purpose. You have to be on track with living your vision. The reason I put it like this is because many of us know things. Sit a bunch of men in a room and have them talk about what they know, and soon the room is full of advice, 'wisdom,' and knowledge up to the eyeballs. Ask most men for advice, about what you should do, and you're going to get an earful, for sure. Being on track with your purpose means that you don't just know your purpose – you're also acting and living it. You're not just seeing a vision for yourself and your life; you are actually living that vision. You're doing stuff, you're cultivating the elements of your life that you want to grow. You're moving down your road.

Being on track doesn't mean that you've nailed it. It doesn't mean that you've achieved your dream, graduated from the program, or accomplished whatever you need to complete for your purpose to be fully realized. 'Being on track' means just that: Your actions, words, thoughts, and feelings are moving in alignment – on track – with your vision. It's the opposite of being dis-tracted. Being on track means that you are making some kind of positive forward movement toward realizing your purpose.

It can be very incremental but, however small the steps, if you're truly moving in the direction of your vision, you'll have this Key in place. It's about walking your talk. It's about knowing and following your swadharma. So if you discover that you're in the wrong career, and you might have married the wrong person, and you're living in the wrong city, you don't have to get a new job, get divorced, and move to another town before you have this Key. Being on track with your vision means you just have to be moving in that direction. It means you're exploring other career options, you're getting your resumé together. It means you're trying to have some honest dialogue with your wife, or you're seeking out a relationship expert, or looking for a divorce lawyer. You're visiting other cities. Do you get the idea? You get this Key when you start to move out of your misalignment with your purpose and vision and into a better alignment. Little moves make a huge difference. You let the universe know you're sincere when you take this kind of action. Even small actions can demonstrate commitment.

Slow is Smooth and Smooth is Fast

Being on track also means making some progress. It can take some time, even years, to right your path if you're really off. I don't recommend blowing up your life in an impulsive manner. Doing that kind of thing causes a lot of pain, breaks a lot of shit, and leaves some men damaged and traumatized. Some men freak out and try to change too much too fast and get burned; they then give up and go back to the easier Black Road way of being.

Steady progress, guided by wisdom, is the best way to move. 'Slow is Smooth and Smooth is Fast' is something I've learned from men who are elite military operators. If we try to bulldoze our way too hard to our Truth, we can stir up a lot of unnecessary obstacles and make a lot of noise. It isn't always the best way.

Going too fast can be sloppy and messy, but you also have to be alert and vigilant that you don't go too slowly or get stuck. You don't want to be a coward and always take the smallest possible action to stay safe – or to be lazy and make half-hearted token gestures. Make your actions as strong as you can: that's what we mean by being on track. Doing what you can, not more and not less.

This is where a coach or a mentor and/or a men's group can be super helpful. They'll let you know if you've been talking about a change for too long without actually walking toward it. They'll push you if you are going too slow or playing small, and they'll tell you to chill out if you're pushing too hard or running your engine too hot. Having other men in your life who are into this work helps a lot – we pace each other, we push each other, and give shelter to each other when the road gets hard. This First Key is not to be done in isolation. It's way more effective and way more fun to have other Red Road walkers involved in the process.

Backbone

Trial and Error

Men don't like to be wrong. Men don't like to give up. We don't like to own up that we're lost and ask for directions. We don't like to admit that we've failed. This distaste for failure and the wish to avoid the 'agony of defeat' can be a real block for some of us. When we are afraid of coming up with the 'wrong' vision or – worse yet – finding our purpose but failing to fulfill it, we get paralyzed. This kind of fear is what stops most men from even daring to dream or consider their purpose and vision. If this is the case for you, get over it. The only way we learn the lessons of life is through trial and error. Just admitting that you need growth, or change, or help is a huge step.

'My way isn't working.'

'I hate my life.'

'I want something different, but I'm afraid I can't have it.'

'I need help.'

To say any of these can be a challenge for a red-blooded man, but, you know what? Suck it up. Go there if you need to. It's the only way forward.

Success is Messy.

T. Harv Ecker

The path to wholeness and real happiness for a man is almost never a straight one. We need to be ready from the outset to fail, fall, get up, and go again. Sometimes this is called 'falling forward.' On the Red Road, you will have to adjust your course again and again. The process of finding your purpose and staying on track with your vision usually requires a ton of trial and error. Be willing to get messy if you want to own this Key.

FIND YOUR PURPOSE, CREATE YOUR VISION

If you don't already know your purpose, then your first purpose is totally clear. Until you know what your purpose is, your purpose in life is to find your purpose!

So how do we go about finding our purpose, or checking to determine if our current purpose is still really true? Sometimes it's as simple as looking at what we're very good at or what we most love in life. Sometimes it's a little more complicated. Sometimes we need to look at what we really care about, what we're passionate about. I sometimes have my students answer the questions: What is it that really breaks your heart open? When you're old and looking back on your life, or when you're on your deathbed, what do you think will really matter to you?

Sometimes our purpose is a contribution that we're meant to make. Ask yourself what your 'gift' is. What are you uniquely gifted with? What is that you have that is most valuable to offer your world? It might be a talent or some kind of professional skill. It may be a unique passion of some sort. It can be some kind of life experience you've been gifted with that makes you unique. In some cases, a man's gift comes from his wounds: the traumas and trials that he's lived through and healed. In most men, their purpose is an mixture of all of these things.

For many men, part of our purpose comes from what we're born into, or what we live into. Most men play key roles in families, societies, and communities. A man's deep purpose isn't just about what he does for work. In the chapter on the inner King Power in Part 2, I will take you through a powerful exercise to help you be clear about your purpose,

> Until you find your true purpose, your purpose is to find your true purpose.

45

but remember that sometimes it takes time – even with the best exercise in a book. Remember, until you find your true purpose, your purpose is to find your true purpose.

Fatherhood

As a father, and as the son of an absent father, I've got to include a section here about fatherhood. If you have kids – even if they're grown up – part of your true purpose as a man is to be an excellent father. Period. Ultimately, we all seek to be excellent in all of our connections to life, but the role we play with our children as their dad is something that deserves special attention and focus. We have a lot in this book about fathering and fatherhood. It's one of the most common occupations for men, and one of the hardest to do really well. It deserves a tremendous amount of focus and attention and commitment. On their deathbed, men with kids consistently say the most important thing is what they did or didn't do for their children. If you have kids, whatever it takes, if you want to be deeply powerful and free, invest your heart in your fathering.

What is your Passion?

The clarity of your vision and purpose is important; we need to know clearly where we're going. It's also important that our purpose has some fire, some passion. We need to be passionate about our vision so that we have the fuel we need to keep going. It has to move us. We have to care deeply about our purpose. We have to want our vision with an intensity – almost an urgency. The visions and purposes that really propel us are the ones that we *have* to realize.

Anthony Robbins likes to say that change happens when it becomes a 'must,' not just a 'should' – like when we can't tolerate a bad situation anymore and we need to change it or else suffer. Your passionate vision can be like that. With a little work, and if you follow the stuff I lay out for you in this book, you can be so on fire with love for your life and your vision that you *must* live it, you must walk the Red Road. In the beginning, your vision may be a 'getting away from pain' vision. It may be that, for now, your passion is about getting free from your Black Road bullshit and the agony of living away from your Truth. That's good fuel too. That's just another kind of passion. It's the passion that a man feels for air when he's held underwater.

With luck, your passion will soon enough be 'I love my vision,' but whatever the case, you need it. You need that powerful fiery fuel. It gives you a rootedness on your path. Without passion, without that intensity and heart connection to our mission, we get robbed by all things waiting to distract us and drain our energy. Have you seen Michelangelo's painting of the torment of St Anthony? It shows an elderly St Anthony surrounded by demons and monsters pulling on him and clawing him from all sides. It's a potent image of a man trying to stay focused on his vision. Where St Anthony has demons, we have money pressures, relationship dramas, body energy issues, and the general noise of modern life to contend with as we move down our road. If we don't have vision, or our vision is weak, those demons are going to win. Remember the last time you really had to take a leak? Did you find a place to piss? You sure did! It may seem silly, but that kind of urgency is what I'm talking about.

When you zero in on and articulate a vision for your life that turns you on so much that *you have to live it*, then you're on to something! Not only does that kind of purpose stand a better chance of getting realized, it also is much more fun. Then reaching your purpose doesn't feel like work. It feels like life. We want to wake up in the morning knowing where we're going and feeling great about going there.

Pay Attention to You

Like most of the tools in this book, the process of getting your First Key and finding your deep purpose takes introspection. It requires you to slow down a little bit and learn how to listen to your deeper truer self. You need to be with yourself and do the digging that you need to do to get down into your heart, down beneath the haze and distractions of your mind. You need to get beyond what everyone else wants from you, what your dad wanted from you, what you think women want from you. You need to find out what *you want from you*, what you want to get from life and what you want to give to your life. Find what it is that you *have* to give to life, what you really long for.

Your purpose is what gets you out of bed in the morning and keeps you going through your days — the vision that guides your decisions. When you're clear about your deep purpose in life and you're on track with living your vision, you're holding in your hand the First Key.

SUMMING IT UP

The First Key — know your true purpose in life, and be on track with living your vision.

Dharma — this is an ancient Sanskrit word which can be summarized as the all-pervading natural force that keeps the universe in check, and everything interacting perfectly in the natural world.

Swadharma — this means 'one's own dharma' — our place in the whole universal order.

Live True — this is one of the core philosophies of the work we do together. When you really know yourself and live the truth of who you are, and you're connected to that deep natural force of dharma, little or nothing can stop you.

Be on Track with your Purpose – it is the difference between knowing what your purpose is and actually taking action toward it. Get on track.

BRUTAL HONESTY

Take a moment away from the flow of your life to sit quietly with a notebook or journal. Center yourself by closing your eyes and breathing a little deeply. When you feel centered and somewhat quiet inside simply ask yourself these questions and write down the answers that come. You might do all of the questions first by writing out everything that comes to you, like a long rant. Then go back through it and try to answer each question in three sentences or less.

- What gets me out of bed in the morning?
- What do I spend most of my energy on in life?
- What do I love most in life?
- How would I spend my time if I only had one year to live?
- What unique gifts do I have to offer the world?
- If I knew I couldn't fail, what life path would I attempt?
- What is my deep purpose in life?

At this stage, the questions aren't really meant to get crystal-clear answers. In fact, it's good if these questions just stir you up a little bit.

Later, in the chapter on King Power, I will take you through a focused process so you can get super clear on your purpose, your core values, and your vision for your life.

Now that we've explored the First Key in detail, in the next chapter we'll look at the Second Key, cultivating a deep and authentic spiritual connection.

4

THE SECOND KEY

*Stop telling God how big your problems are, and
start telling your problems how big your God is.*

Bumper sticker

The Second Key: Cultivate a deep and authentic spiritual connection.

Every man I've ever known who has real backbone has some kind of spiritual connection, something that works for him that he uses on a regular basis to inspire, empower, and ground himself on his path. This Second Key connects us to the power of the universe, the power of the Great Spirit that creates, sustains, and moves all things.

This key is worded in a specific way: *cultivate a deep and authentic spiritual connection.* Let's look first at the word 'spiritual.' I use it a lot in my teaching and I use it consciously. Spiritual doesn't mean religious. It doesn't need to have anything to do with any formal religion or with anyone else's idea about

God or religion either. A deep and authentic spiritual connection can be with 'Spirit,' like the Great Spirit, or God, or some idea of the Universal Power, etc. But it is also very important that there is a connection with *your* spirit. By 'spirit' here, I mean your essence, the soul of you. Your deep heart and inner workings. For most men who have the Second Key, it's a combination of both the universal and the inner sense of Spirit.

My first experience of cultivating a spiritual connection came when I was a teenage drug addict trying to get sober. If you look at the 12 Steps of Alcoholics Anonymous, you'll see that six of the steps mention God directly, and one more mentions a 'spiritual awakening.' At that point in my path, I wanted nothing to do with 'God.' I was a card-carrying non-conformist and had a strong distaste for any kind of institution – especially any religious institution. The elders of AA – really my first spiritual mentors – were mostly crusty, hardcore, redneck men who had been around the block more than once. Some of them had done time. None of them minced words. 'God can be whatever you need it to be – 's long as it helps you stay sober! Religion is about saving your soul, spirituality is about saving your ass.'

They made it clear to me in no uncertain terms that my ideas about God were insignificant compared to my need for help. They had me there. I was pretty miserable and fairly desperate. I was only 17 at the time, and I lived with both my parents, who were still drinking and using. The elders advised me to 'just start prayin' and see what happens.'

One afternoon I went for a walk in the woods behind my house. The woods have always been a sort of sanctuary for me. I walked up to the edge of a big wooded valley and then sat down on a log. I tried to pray. The praying felt fake, and I felt stupid. I remembered hearing someone in a meeting once say that you could pray for a sign if you weren't sure what you were doing, so

I tried that. 'If there's anything out there, show me. Just give me a sign.' I sat for a moment, feeling stupid, and then – and I shit you not – a giant and majestic red-tailed hawk flew over where I was sitting, under the canopy of trees, not more than 10 feet over my head. I could hear its wings cutting through the air. The hawk landed on a branch less than 30 feet away from where I was and just perched there. I shifted a little bit to see it better – I must have made a noise. The hawk jumped off the branch, spread its massive wings, and soared down into the valley with sunlight on its wings. I was astounded and felt massively blessed. Every hair stood up on my body. My heart stirred inside my chest. I'd got a sign. I was never able to relate to the version of God that they talked about in church, but the vision of that hawk in the woods that day was exactly the sign that I needed. I learned to connect to 'a power greater than myself' that I felt no pressure to define or name. I started praying daily and eventually added sitting meditation to my routine. But I never got into spirituality because it was cool, or because it was fun, or because my friends were doing it. I didn't seek a spiritual connection to save my soul or to be a good boy. I sought the connection with Spirit to save my ass, to give me the strength I needed as I walked the path of recovery and healing. I am proud to say that it worked. As of this moment, I've clocked in more than 25 years clean and sober. The only person in my family to do so. Your spiritual connection can be – actually, it has to be – on your terms.

No Bullshit Spirituality

For most men – especially regular men – to relate to spirituality, it has to be totally real. For men to buy into a spiritual discipline or system, it has to make sense to them and also produce results. There are all kinds of reasons to follow a religious path or stay faithful to some kind of set of beliefs, but when it comes to walking toward wholeness and deep happiness, you need to err on the side of authenticity. Your spiritual connection must be authentic. It has to be true for you. There's only one person who can say if your connection is true, and that's not me or Billy Graham or the Pope or Deepak Chopra. Those wise geezers at AA were really good.

'It don't matter what you think God is, as long as you know it ain't you!' Start with what you can relate to. The way the Second Key is stated invites you to cultivate a deep and authentic connection with Spirit. There's no pressure to have it all figured out, it's a cultivation. You can wade into the process bit by bit.

MAKE IT DEEP

The word 'deep' here means that it's a deep-felt thing. The connection has an impact. It's an actual felt connection instead of a mere belief. It's not just a box we tick on a form. The connection isn't something we just have in our head: we have it in our heart, in our body, in our balls. Deep also means that whatever you're doing for your spiritual practice is actually working. If you're meditating to keep yourself centered, then it should be actually keeping you centered. If you're spending time praying, or doing whatever spiritual practice suits you, it should be giving you some actual results. Deep means you're not just dabbling. It means you're not just showing up, sitting in the back row with your arms folded. Deep and authentic mean that you're really putting yourself into it. Sometimes men feel like they are being un-manly if they are too sincere. If we are to get this Second Key, we need to drop that kind of belief.

Spirituality is one of those things that has been largely abdicated to the women in our lives. Often, the female in a relationship is 'the spiritual one,' while the male is the 'practical one.' When I was focusing more squarely on teaching meditation, most of my students were women. If you go to almost any spiritual weekend, retreat, or workshop – except mine – you'll see the same thing: a room full of women, with a few effeminate 'spiritual guys' and maybe one or two reluctant husbands who were dragged in, grumpy and resistant. That's why the authentic part is so important. We just won't do it if it seems too hokey, or if we're there to please someone else.

FIRE IN OUR BELLIES

Sam Keen's *Fire in the Belly* was one of the first men's books I ever read. I love that title and that image: *Fire in the Belly*! The kind of deep and authentic spiritual connection I'm referring to in the Second Key is something that inspires us – literally. The word 'inspiration' means to be filled with spirit. I think of blowing on a coal to make it produce fire, or breathing air into someone's lungs, bringing them to life when they have drowned. When we have an authentic spiritual connection, we have access to a powerful source of energy that is beyond our mind, beyond our day-to-day life. It's right there inside us like a fire in our belly. It's all around us in nature, in the universe, in the hearts of others. When we've done the work to cultivate this connection and have cultivated it in a profound way, the connection can be a tremendous source of support and constant guidance. Step 11 of Alcoholics Anonymous reads: 'We sought through prayer and meditation to improve our conscious contact with God as we understood Him, praying only for the knowledge of His will for us and the power to carry that out.' Conscious contact, knowledge, power – important things to have on the Red Road.

The way you embrace this Second Key doesn't even need to be about 'God' or anything that is outside yourself. In the more personal awareness practices like meditation, 'spirituality' is not about connecting to 'spirits' or anything supernatural, it's an inner hygiene practice. It's like washing your heart or cleansing the crap off of your awareness. We learn to peel away the layers that are between us and our experience of life. Without this sort of practice, we're living life as if we're taking a shower with a raincoat on. We're not totally there, so life is not totally touching us, and we're not totally touching life either. Our authentic spiritual practice brings us into an intimate connection with our life, with life itself, in all of life's forms: people, nature, and, yes – also sometimes what some people would call God.

If you already have a connection to God or a belief system, cultivating your spiritual connection gives you a deeper, more tactile experience of your faith. If you don't have a connection to God, or even if you're totally against religion and spiritual ideas, cultivating a spiritual practice can help you make a connection to something greater, something beyond yourself. But when you meditate, pray, or practice from the heart – when you do it in the no-bullshit, in-your-bones way I'm talking about – you're not improving your conscious contact with someone else's understanding of God, religion, or Spirit. It's yours. It's your own bona fide connection.

YOUR WAY

Mind you, your version of an authentic connection doesn't even need to include prayer or meditation or anything that looks typically spiritual. It could be something totally different. This is one of the mistakes of the New Age wellness industries. They have a hard time marketing to men, partly because they only offer very rigid ideas about what constitutes a spiritual practice. It was no coincidence that I had my initial breakthrough in the woods. Many men get spiritually connected spending time in nature. The word GOD could be an acronym for the Great Out Doors. I know so many men who get their spiritual connection fishing, hunting, or motorcycling. One of my riding buddies, a veteran NYPD detective, once said about church, 'I'd rather be sitting on my motorcycle thinking about God than sitting in church thinking about my motorcycle.' I have some of my best meditations sitting on my Harley.

What constitutes 'spiritual' is really in the heart of the man who is making the connection. Anything can be spiritual when we approach it with the intent of making this connection.

Also, men are more likely to connect spiritually alone, in solitude, rather than in a group such as a yoga class, self-help workshop, or retreat. This is one of the nice things about motorcycling. Even if we're riding in a group, we're alone while we're moving. I think of the classic image of a dad outside by himself, hose in hand, watering his lawn. He's probably doing a kind of simple meditation practice. Of course, on our path, we're not just talking about spacing out while watering the lawn. We're talking about investing some time, energy, and creative thought in our practice. Design a potent practice that suits your own lives and needs.

CONNECT YOUR PRACTICE WITH YOUR PURPOSE

The main thing that is going to help you to create your own masculine paradigm for spiritual connection is the First Key. Men generally don't connect to Spirit well unless there's a clear purpose behind it. Spend time getting to know your purpose, and the spiritual connection will come easier. It will be clear what you're praying about – if you're praying – or why you're meditating, if you're doing that. One of the military men I worked with in my veterans' program got hooked on meditation, not because of anything it did for his mind, but for the way it helped his workouts. He found that when he took time to connect with Spirit using meditation, he was able to kick ass in his PT drills. This way, his spiritual connection was in service to his higher vision of being a fit and fearsome warrior. You know the time you spend doing spiritual discipline is time well spent if you know it's keeping you on track with your vision.

Later, in the chapter about the Mystic, we will have more specific suggestions for practices and ways you can get connected. For now, have a look at your current connection to Spirit.

SUMMING IT UP

The Second Key – cultivate a deep and authentic spiritual connection

Authentic – for most men – especially 'regular' men – to relate to spirituality, it has be to totally real, no bullshit.

Spiritual – in the context of our work together, spiritual doesn't mean religious. A deep and authentic spiritual connection can be with 'Spirit' such as the Great Spirit, or God, or some idea of the Universal Power, etc.

Deep – the spiritual connection is something that you actually *feel* rather than something you just believe in.

Inspiring – the kind of deep and authentic spiritual connection that we are working toward in this book is something that inspires us, something that puts 'fire in our belly.' (The word inspiration means to be filled with spirit.)

Find your Way – your version of an authentic connection doesn't even need to include prayer or meditation, or anything that looks typically spiritual. It could be spending time in nature, chopping wood, riding a motorcycle, etc.

BRUTAL HONESTY

Take a moment away from the flow of your life to sit quietly with a notebook or journal. Center yourself by closing your eyes and breathing a little deeper. When you feel centered and somewhat quiet inside, simply ask yourself these questions and write down the answers that come. There are no right or wrong answers, just true or untrue. Remember, this is for you.

- Do you have a spiritual connection, religious faith, or spiritual practice currently?
- If so, what does it do for you? Does it help you to stay on track with your purpose?
- If you don't currently have a spiritual connection, what are some practices that you can think of that would help you to cultivate a spiritual connection?
- How might a deeper spiritual connection serve your purpose and help you be more on track with your vision?

PRACTICAL SUGGESTION

Begin including some quiet contemplative time in your day. It could take the form of prayer, meditation, or walking. You can use this time to reflect quietly on your vision, or even to mentally imagine yourself living your vision. As you read on through the book, I will give you more suggested practices to enhance your connection, but for now, start setting the time and energy aside and see what happens.

Now that we have looked at how cultivating a deep spiritual connection is one of the essential elements of developing your backbone, in the next chapter we will look at what has been holding you back in life so far – in other words, your bullshit.

5

THE THIRD KEY

Liberty, when it begins to take root, is a plant of rapid growth.

George Washington

The Third Key: Get free from your bullshit. You can be as clear as can be about your purpose and your vision, and super connected to Spirit within and without, but if you don't do what you need to do to clean up the messes in your life, handle your addictions, and clear out your inner baggage, the best you can hope for is very slow progress.

Often times, this chapter is the one that will make or break a man on his path to creating true, lasting progress. Fail to get free from your bullshit and you will be thwarted and drained and bound by your bullshit. Get free from your bullshit and you become incredibly powerful – almost superhuman. The strength of your backbone is proportional to the degree of freedom you enjoy from your bullshit.

What is your bullshit? Your bullshit is made up of all the ways you're not living your truth. You're in your bullshit when you're not using your backbone, when you forget or betray what you stand for. What do you really believe is the best way to think, speak, act, and live? This is your Truth. Your bullshit is the opposite of all that. Why do I call it bullshit? Because it's not really you. Your bullshit elements are like layers covering the real you. Remember the idea of becoming Wildmen? We are not sculpting ourselves into something 'better'; we're taking away what doesn't work, shedding the layers of bad conditioning, unconscious behavior, and disempowered choices. On this path, we are making a bet that underneath all of that, you are big and powerful and good. All of that power, that wisdom, and that excellence is your true nature. All you have to do is carve away and drop the bullshit.

Michelangelo said that when he carved a marble sculpture, like the magnificent David, he did it by looking at the block of marble and 'seeing' the figure within it. Then, he said, his job was simply to remove everything else that wasn't the figure. Let's use that as our vision for transformation. We're just taking away what we don't need – the bullshit – to reveal the wild, powerful man that you really are.

INNIES AND OUTIES

Sometimes a man's bullshit is obvious. Some of us have the kind of gross character defects, bad habits, and personality flaws that people can see from a block away. Sometimes our flaws are a lot more subtle. I've noticed that men generally tend to fall into two camps: 'innies' and 'outies.' Like belly buttons that either poke out or go in, a man is usually either an innie – someone who keeps their bullshit hidden under wraps and is able to behave himself, play well with others, etc. – or an outie – everybody knows if there's something wrong with this kind of guy. If he's angry, or deranged, or otherwise 'off' – everybody knows it. Of the two, I am definitely an outie. Us outies have a hard time if we don't handle our bullshit. We tend to make enemies, get fired, get dumped, and even get locked up more often than the 'innies,' who might be just as messed up, but no one knows it because they keep it inside.

DON'T TAKE YOURSELF TOO SERIOUSLY

Before we wade any further into the bullshit, I want to repeat something I said in the Introduction. One of the greatest abilities a man can develop on the spiritual path is the ability to laugh at his own ego's antics. When dealing with your bullshit, it's super important to have a sense of humor. It's essential that you learn to take all of your bullshit with a grain of salt. We've all got some, and it's all pretty shitty. But if you can learn to 'pan out' a little bit and see yourself like a character in a movie, you might be able to see the stupid things you do, think, and say and laugh at yourself a little bit. This is a good way to give yourself self-love in a masculine way. Of course, there are lots of ways to love yourself and we will delve deeper into that later, but for now, try not to get defensive or too serious about practicing this Key.

PROGRESS NOT PERFECTION

The other thing that we need to get clear here is that we aren't talking about totally eliminating all bullshit. The key to real happiness and power is to *get free* from your bullshit. The bullshit will still be there to some degree, no matter how great we are and how Red Road we become. There's a great little section that comes from the chapter in AA's self-titled *Alcoholics Anonymous* called 'How it Works,' which says:

> We are not saints. No one among us has been able to maintain anything like perfect adherence to these principles. The point is that we are willing to grow along spiritual lines. We claim spiritual progress rather than spiritual perfection.

This is what we're looking for in our quest to be free from our bullshit: progress toward freedom. Like being on track with our vision — we need only to be moving in the direction of freedom to have this Key.

There are three main kinds of bullshit that we need to get free from: Mental Bullshit, Body Bullshit, and Life Bullshit.

MENTAL BULLSHIT

Mental Bullshit is really the biggest one. The Life Bullshit and Body Bullshit are really rooted in the mind. Your Mental Bullshit consists of four main kinds of BS: bad conditioning, inner wounds, limiting beliefs, and triggers. This is the stuff that is somewhat 'hard-wired' in you, meaning it's not just attitudinal. Your Mental Bullshit can't be shifted simply by thinking a better thought or getting an 'attitude adjustment.' The Mental Bullshit is what stays after the adjustment wears off. You can think of your Mental Bullshit as the ground that your momentary attitudes and feelings and reactions spring out of. Let's look at each of the four kinds of Mental Bullshit.

Bad Conditioning

By bad conditioning I mean the way we were trained to be from a very young age. I don't want to get into a whole lot of psycho-babble here, but it's important to look back at the way we were raised and know what kind of training we got. Small kids do a whole lot of adaptation based on their environment. Our neurology – meaning our brains and nervous systems – wire themselves according to what we're exposed to, especially in our first five to seven years. Little ones just want love from the grown-ups, like plants need sun and water. And, like a plant growing toward the light, a kid will grow toward love and affection, and grow away from anger, etc. If the grown-ups are overwhelmed, the kid might grow into an out-of-the-way, low-maintenance kid. If the parents are depressed, the kid might become a clown or a cheerer upper. Kids might make themselves 'bigger' to get attention or 'smaller' to avoid harmful attention.

There are many kinds of conditioning. Most of our conditioning is necessary to help us be effective, normal, functioning people in the world. Inuit kids are conditioned to live their Inuit lives. City kids are conditioned for their lives in the city. The entire time we're growing up we're being conditioned. Our conditioning becomes Mental Bullshit when it's bad conditioning – the kind of conditioning that trains us to be fearful, or timid, or self-harming. It's the kind of training that teaches us to not live fully, to not be authentic or express ourselves. Conditioning gets stronger over time. The more we act, think, and speak from our conditioning, the stronger the conditioning gets. With bad conditioning, this snowball effect can eventually cripple a man and keep him from ever realizing his real purpose.

We're not going to get into all the possible kinds of conditioning and give you ways to combat each specific type of conditioning here. There are all kinds of techniques out there and some of them can be very helpful. Let's just say that to be free from your bad conditioning, you need to have a sense of what that conditioning is and be aware when you're reinforcing it. The questions at the end of this chapter will help you to take a deeper look, and the rest of this book will give you tools so that you can 'live your way' out of your bad conditioning.

Inner Wounds

Inner wounds are also part of our conditioning, but they can affect us a little differently. Some inner wounds are the result of being deeply hurt or violated by others, or the result of some natural calamity such as a storm, a disease, or other external event such as a war. Some wounds come from painful life experiences like big failures or relationship breakdowns. Inner wounds are the hurts we can't let go of. They are the things that take the form of permanent weaknesses, like a leg injury that causes us to limp for the rest of our life. But they're not physical, they're in our heart. Inner wounds will live in us and emit a bad feeling or cause the absence of feeling – numbness. They make us believe we're no good or they make us afraid to take chances. Sometime in the past we were wounded and we recoiled, but we never stood up straight again. Our inner wounds from the past warp our experience of the present. Some men weave their whole lives around their inner wounds. They choose careers from their wounds; they choose their marriages from their wounds. Their wounds are also what bring down their careers and marriages – and more. If we are to be free and able to live our deeply happy, powerful lives, we need to deal with our inner wounds.

Some inner wounds are healed simply by acknowledging them. Others require you to do some deeper work. Some wounds require professional help. Growing up in an alcoholic family left me with some deep inner feelings of unworthiness. My parents were drunk and checked-out; in lots of ways, I was neglected for much of my young life. It took many deep sessions with a gifted psychotherapist to get me to the point where I could get out from under them. Practices like meditation can also be great for healing and managing inner wounds. Much of the work I do with people one-on-one is aimed at helping to heal and manage inner wounds. Notice that I say 'heal' and 'manage.' Some wounds are really here to stay; they're not meant to be obliterated. They are part of what makes us who we are. Sometimes healing means they go away, and sometimes healing means changing our relationship with them. The goal is to be free from them, no longer ruled by them. Instead of being swamped by them, or defining who we are by them, we can look at them, accept them, and learn from them. Our wounds can help us to serve others and, ultimately, make us stronger men.

> *Whatever doesn't kill me makes me stronger.*
> Friedrich Nietzsche

Stop the Replay

Inner wounds have the same snowball effect that any conditioning has. The more we live with the wounds in an unconscious way, the deeper and stronger they get. One of the ways we reinforce our inner wounds is by mentally replaying the events and feelings associated with them. The more we replay our wounding moments and retell the stories in our head, the more they become permanent parts of who we are. The things that wounded us were just events that happened to us. They only happened as many times as they actually did, but we relive and replay the events thousands of times in our thoughts. Someone calls a boy 'faggot' on the playground. On the playground it happened only once, but how many times will the boy replay that 'faggot' in his head? Over and over again, we replay the painful words and moments of our life and let them gain gigantic proportions.

The more potent the inner wound is, the more power it has to pull our attention out of the now and back into that replay. Unexamined wounds tend to make it hard for us to be present in our life. They use up our energy reserves and our heart's feeling bandwidth. We're too busy feeling some old pain to feel any of the goodness that is around us. We're too busy focusing on the mistakes and wounds of our past life to avoid the mistakes and wounds that are threatening us in the now. When our inner wounds are not in check, we live partly in the past. It's as if there is a part of us there, trapped like a ghost.

One potent practice for dealing with inner wounds is to tell the stories about what wounded you somewhere outside your head. Write the stories down in a 'just the facts ma'am' sort of reporting style. Make sure to include what was happening before the wounding thing happened and also play the story forward past the point of trauma. Try to tell it like this: 'I was playing kickball at recess. I missed a kick and Jason, the cool kid, called me a faggot. The other kids laughed and I was humiliated. Then we finished the game and recess was over. I went back in the school building, washed my face, and went to math class.' Don't just say: 'Jason called me a faggot. I was humiliated.' We tend to replay only the dramatic part in our minds. Putting it in context really helps to lessen the intensity and power of the wound. You can also try speaking the stories out loud to a trusted man friend or even in your men's group, or to a counselor. Taking the time really to examine what wounded you, especially when you look at the broader context, can help to lessen its grip on you.

And, of course, I know that when we talk about our inner wounds, we are not just talking about our somebody-called-me-a-faggot moments. Some of our inner wounds come from gnarly life circumstances like incest, abuse, neglect, violence, combat, death, and betrayal. Some of us are gay and have been called faggots our whole life. Some of us have been in combat, or prison. Only you know how severe this aspect of your Mental Bullshit is. Get the help that you need. There's nothing unmanly about getting help from a professional. If you do, just make sure they know what your intentions are and what your vision for yourself as a man is.

Limiting Beliefs

Limiting beliefs are the beliefs we have about ourselves and our life that are ... well ... limiting. Every man has a philosophy, a belief system that he lives according to. I'm not talking about Christian, Muslim, Hindu, or atheist beliefs here. We see life through the lens of our general beliefs about life. And, if we haven't consciously done the work we're doing here to critically examine the beliefs we live by, chances are our beliefs have just crept in there. Or we've adopted other people's beliefs. Or we have created our beliefs in reaction to other people's beliefs. Many of us either have beliefs just like our dad's, or we have the opposite beliefs to our dad. Either way, we're living in bullshit because we're not choosing the way we believe and see the world. Limiting beliefs come in two main forms: general and specific.

General limiting beliefs go like this:
Life is hard
People will always let you down
My (race/religion/ethnicity) is the (supreme/best/worst/most
    unfortunate)
Rich people are assholes

Poor people are lazy
Women will trap you
Life is about sacrifice
Deep happiness is impossible
Real men don't cry
Power corrupts
Real happiness is for men who never make mistakes

Specific limiting beliefs go like this:
I am bad with money
My best years are behind me
I can't have everything I want
I am not a good communicator
Because I failed in one marriage, I will probably fail in the next
I was born for bad luck
My unhappiness is because of (my parents/my wife/my job/
    my government)
I am unsuccessful because I am in an unfair situation
My (wife/friend/family member/co-worker/boss) is an asshole
    and will never change
I can't afford to live my dream
Because of my past sins/failures, I don't deserve to be happy

If you read through the two lists, you can easily see how this form of Mental Bullshit holds us back. If you believe 'real happiness is for people who never make mistakes' (and most people do believe that), your chances of attaining deep happiness are next to nothing. If you believe that 'Because I failed in one marriage, I will probably fail in the next,' what kind of husband do you think you'll be? Do you think you will ever be truly powerful if you believe that you are 'unsuccessful because you are in an unfair situation'? Not a chance.

Getting Free from Limiting Beliefs
The key to getting free from this type of Mental Bullshit is mostly awareness. If you look at any area of your life that you are stuck in, I promise you will find at least one limiting belief there. Once you identify the belief and are able to label it bullshit, it has less power over you. This gives you the ability to make choices and live your life based on your vision, based on wisdom.

Sometimes it can be useful to write out a list of your limiting beliefs and really look at them. Then make a parallel list of counter-beliefs that are unlimiting or liberating beliefs to counteract the limiting ones. General limiting beliefs usually can be counteracted by calling them bullshit and affirming something wiser and truer. So, when you find yourself thinking, 'Deep happiness is impossible,' you can just say, 'That's bullshit. I am on the path to deep happiness.' Or if you catch yourself believing, 'Real men don't cry,' you can tell yourself, 'That's bullshit. Real men experience all real human emotions.'

Specific limiting beliefs are more personal and situational, so we need to hit back at them with wiser beliefs on a case-by-case basis. Many specific limiting beliefs are just old, stupid, untrue curses that we have learned to live under. 'I was born for bad luck' or 'My best years are behind me.' These are just total bullshit. It's good to be aware of them and totally dismiss them when they arise.

Sometimes our specific limiting beliefs are not completely bullshit. It may be true that we're not a good communicator. It may be that we are bad with money, or that our boss acts like an asshole. The medicine here is to correct the absoluteness of the belief. Instead of 'I am a bad communicator,' you can say, 'Up until now, I have been a poor communicator. I need to work on that.' Or 'I need to learn how to manage money. Up until now I've been bad at it.' Do you see how 'Up until now ...' sets you free? They are three magical words that free you up to move forward on your Red Road. Instead of being cursed with conditions, we find ourselves embracing learning opportunities. Instead of 'My boss is an asshole,' you can say, 'Up until now, I haven't been able to have a good opinion of my boss. It's hard for me to see him as anything but an asshole.' This puts you in the driver's seat; you're no longer a victim. When our boss is an asshole, there's nothing that we can do: we just have to live with it. When we see that we have a limiting belief, the power shifts into our hands.

Triggers

Triggers are inputs that will consistently create an unwanted emotional and mental reaction. Someone brings up a topic or acts in a certain way, or we encounter something that we have a history with, and – *click* – we're triggered. We're angry, sad, threatened, or paranoid. It's not a choice. When we're triggered, we go into a sort of a trance. It's a kind of conditioned response. Like Pavlov's dogs slobbering when they hear the dinner bell, our response to our trigger is almost unavoidable. Our triggers are the result of our bad conditioning, limiting beliefs, and inner wounds. All of the different kinds of Mental Bullshit gang up and act like little bombs in us, waiting to go off and ruin our day. Men have anger triggers, shame triggers, sadness triggers, fear triggers, and nasty combo triggers that make all of the above flare up in an instant.

Here's a simple example: Your wife asks you a simple question about money, 'Honey, do we have enough in the joint account to cover the car payment?' An innocent yes-or-no question, but you have a trigger about financial insecurity. For whatever reason, because of whatever wounds you have around money, and whatever beliefs you're operating under, you hear the question, get triggered, feel threatened, challenged, and defensive, and you totally overreact. All she did was ask a simple question about money. Now you're in a fight about all of her spending habits, all of your work pressures, all of your financial pain and fear. Your trigger set off the pain bomb. When we get triggered, we get upset and fearful and angry in what seems like an involuntary way. Triggers are irrational. Our triggers are our 'buttons' as in, 'My wife really knows how to push my buttons.' As men trying to walk on the Red Road, we really need to get free from our triggers. All triggers.

There are triggers associated with pleasure too. For instance, most heterosexual men get triggered by the attention of beautiful women. If our sex trigger gets pulled, we will lose our usual discrimination and make decisions we would never normally make. This trigger gets a lot of good men in trouble. This trigger is so reliable that it is used in military espionage. Beautiful female agents seduce their male sources to exploit them for intel – they call it the 'honey trap.' It's so funny to watch the men in our men's retreats get triggered when a good-looking woman comes through our space. A woman comes in and the men change their whole demeanor.

When we're triggered we're blind. We're hoodwinked. Most triggers will make us act like fools, make us give away our power. Sex triggers, anger triggers, pride triggers, respect triggers – when these get pulled we can totally lose ourselves. Some men are full of triggers. These men live in a constantly reactive way. But even having one unexamined trigger makes us weak. If we have a button, someone can push that button and make us lose track of our purpose and betray our vision. No man has the vision to be a triggered, stupid hot-head.

This doesn't mean that we should be totally non-responsive, or always cool-headed. We want to get turned on by beautiful people; we want to be able to be fierce and stand up for ourselves if someone is messing us around. But we want to be able to do it consciously and not just snap into an involuntary trance. Break out of your conditioning, let go of your limiting beliefs, deal with your inner wounds, and your triggers will become fewer and less powerful. All of this is really just an introduction to get you thinking about the bullshit that you carry around inside. You'll be working with a lot of this stuff for your whole life. Compared with the Mental Bullshit, the Body Bullshit and Life Bullshit are no big deal.

BRUTAL HONESTY

Take some time to get quiet with your journal and look deeply at these questions. Don't censor yourself, and remember to have a sense of humor. I suggest going through all the questions once, letting yourself write freely and 'get it all down,' and then going back to zero in on the stuff that seems most important. Remember we are looking for progress, not perfection. These exercises are not to evaluate you; they are to direct you and give you self-knowledge. We'll do the same for Body Bullshit and Life Bullshit later on in this chapter.

- When you take a step back and look at yourself from a mental and emotional point of view, what stands out as the main bullshit that is keeping you from experiencing and living your Truth?
- What kind of bad conditioning and training did you get as a kid? What was the environment like where you grew up? What kind of kid did you have to become to get love or avoid pain? How does this conditioning affect you in your life today?

- What sort of mental wounds do you carry around from your life? What actually happened to cause them? How do these wounds affect you in your life today? What would go better in your life if you were free from these inner wounds? Are there any wounds that you might need professional help with?
- What are your limiting beliefs? Make a list of your top five to ten general and specific limiting beliefs. How do these beliefs affect your life today? What would go better if you didn't have these limiting beliefs? What kind of empowering beliefs can you replace the limiting ones with?
- What are your triggers? What triggers you and what happens when you're triggered? Make a list of these too. How does your triggered behavior affect you and others in your life today? What would go better in your life if you didn't have these triggers?

Once you have identified your Mental Bullshit, you need to make a plan. Knowing your bullshit is one thing, but what are you actually going to do about it? Journaling will get you deeper into understanding your bullshit but the real work starts when you take what you have realized out into your everyday life. If nothing else at this stage, work out what your triggers and your limiting beliefs are, and then look out for them. Make a plan for what you could do differently the next time you are triggered. What will your strategy be? How will you find your backbone in these moments, rather than just giving in to your programming or fate? Like everything we present in this book, it's a process, but one that's well worth it!

BODY BULLSHIT

Body Bullshit is whatever is unconscious and not taken care of in our body. Men have all kinds of things to deal with in their bodies. Our body is an ever-changing living organism. Not all physical challenges are bullshit – I'm not talking about illness or physical ailments. Body Bullshit is the assortment of conditions that arise when we are not taking care of our physical self the way we know we should. Every man needs to attend to his diet, his exercise, his rest, and his wellness, or else all kinds of bullshit can arise that can potentially thwart him on his path.

Food

I'll be damned if I'm going to step into the quagmire of modern dietary advice. For a man walking his Red Road, the most important thing is that you pay attention to what you're eating and pay attention to the effect it has on you. Then, as adult men taking charge of our own lives, we can make choices about what to eat and what not to eat. There's a really bad stereotype about men and food out there. Men get into Body Bullshit when they fall into 'doofus dad' eating habits. We get into trouble when we eat just for weak momentary pleasure or when we eat as a kind of escape. Bad food can act like a mild depressant. Some men seem to keep their power tapped down with shitty, unconscious eating habits. Type 2 diabetes, obesity, fatty liver, sugar addiction ... these types of Body Bullshit afflict way too many men these days. They can be avoided with a little awareness and discipline. How you apply that awareness and discipline is up to you.

The main point here is: pay attention. There are many different food cults and fanatical diet trends out there. Just look at men's fitness websites or magazines. There are all kinds of 'best diets for this and best diets for that' available to learn about. When you know what your deep purpose is, you can decide how you need your body to be, and then go about finding the right nutrition to help your body fulfill your vision. For many men, we eat only what pleases our tongue and don't really do much investigation past that. Along with the taste and convenience of a particular food, start paying attention to how your food makes you feel too. Notice how it affects your mind, your libido, your energy levels. See if your food makes you more or less creative. Notice how it affects your moods. Learn to pay attention to what comes out the other end too. This all may seem really basic – for some men it may be. But I know that, for many men out there, this is a massive growth edge.

Eat Wild

I will offer you this small piece of advice: Think of how wild animals eat, and how lean and strong and sharp they are. They eat what they're meant to eat, and they don't eat more than they need to eat. Their food is always raw, usually very fresh and very simple. I'm not advising that you start eating like a chimpanzee, or in any particular way, but that you just start paying attention. Pay attention to how much processed food and food with lots of artificial ingredients you eat. Personally, as a general rule, I don't like to eat anything with more than six ingredients or anything that has artificial ingredients that I can't easily pronounce. I think our modern society has way too much fake stuff. Because I strive to be an authentic man, I also strive to eat authentic food. I am not a fanatic about any of this. Because of my work I travel a great deal, so often times I have to choose among the least artificial options on a chain-restaurant or airplane menu – no big deal. But when I can choose, and when I look at my overall food consumption, I try to keep it simple, pure, natural, and tasty. Tasty is important.

Slow Down and Pay Attention
In general, try to be more conscious about your eating times. Try to avoid eating while you're on the run. If you have time, pause before you eat to shift from the sympathetic (fight/flight) nervous system to the parasympathetic (relaxation) nervous system. This is a good reason to say grace before you eat. Even if you're not a believer, taking a moment to make this shift can change your whole experience of eating.

Pay attention to the amount you eat and see if you can feel when you're full. Also try chewing your food more and really taste what you're putting in your mouth. Part of being aware of our food is learning to consciously enjoy it. I like to chew my bites at least 30 times before I swallow. If I have time, and I am alone, I chew more. When I chew like this, I always eat less, and feel less tired after a meal.

Try an experiment: Next time you eat your favorite food, slow way down, chew the food and really savor what you're eating. If it's good, you'll enjoy it more. Warning: I wouldn't try this with commercial 'fast food.' Commercial fast food is meant to be eaten fast. If you slow down and really chew and savor your favorite chain burger, you'll probably be disappointed and even disgusted.

Here I'm giving you some of my own practices that I have adopted by paying attention. It's not to say that any way of eating is going to keep you from getting sick. And no diet is going to keep you from dying: 100 per cent of people who eat healthy diets eventually die.

Move your Body

Exercise is the same kind of quagmire as diet. Everyone has an opinion about what to do and how to do it. I'm not getting into any of that here. I'll just say that our modern, civilized life has a very different level of activity than our ancient ancestors' or other wild animals'. In general, we don't need to hunt, gather, harvest, or even really do much to prepare our food. Modern life can afford a man the 'luxury' of sitting on the couch all day, working from home on his laptop, ordering his food to be delivered, and even engaging in virtual activities like combat, sex, and skateboarding with the use of video games and internet porn.

To keep this section on Body Bullshit simple, let's just say *use your body*. Walk, run, play, dance, fuck, climb, lift things, throw things, break a sweat. Do something that makes your heart pound at least a little every day. Pay attention to how many virtual things you do, like internet porn or video games, and balance your virtual adventures with some real ones. These are the minimum recommendations. Don't become an immobile couch potato. If you already have, get off your butt and start to move – whatever that means to you.

If you want to take this to the next level, take the time to craft a vision for your overall fitness. Look at your deep purpose and your vision for life, and ask: What kind of body do I need? How long do I want to live and still be active and strong? Are there things I would like to do with my body but currently can't? Men on the Black Road never ask these questions. They just

Your body is priceless, and not taking care of it is just plain stupid.

lumber along until something breaks down. The idea of getting free from your Body Bullshit is to make all of the aspects of your physical life chosen and conscious. Pay attention to everything you do and don't do, and notice the results. If you do take some kind of exercise, pay attention to its effects. If you don't do much with your body, examine why and also pay attention to the effects of being sedentary. Make sense?

Down Time

Rest and wellness are very important components of a healthy man's physical life too. Some men are the opposite of couch potatoes. They are the non-stop drivers and pushers. This kind of constant grinding takes a toll on the body too. Rest is essential to work into our busy life. Testosterone levels are shown to drop dramatically when men don't get enough sleep at night. But when I say rest, I don't just mean getting enough sleep. I mean paying attention to your stress levels and noticing when you need down time. Wellness practices like restorative yoga, sauna, steam room, and massage are great things to find time to do. Some men find these kinds of practices to be too effeminate, but if you ask any elite athlete they will tell you that the right kind of rest and recovery time is as important for the body as exercise and nutrition. It's better to have conscious rest time than 'zoning out' behaviors like watching TV, smoking weed, and drinking alcohol. These are examples of unconscious down time. See if you can get your rest and relaxation time in without spacing out. Regular meditation, if done with the right attitude, is also a powerful way to help the body restore and renew.

Your body is priceless, and not taking care of it is just plain stupid. You don't have to follow anyone else's standard for physical wellbeing; you can decide for yourself. Be proactive with doctor check-ups, move your body some every day, pay attention to what you're sticking in your pie-hole. The Red Road approach to our bodies is like the Red Road approach to anything else: conscious. Look at your deep purpose and vision, and ask yourself: Given what my vision is, what is the wisest way to treat my body? That question alone will keep you free from a lot of Body Bullshit.

BRUTAL HONESTY

- When you take a step back and look at your body, what stands out as the greatest example of Body Bullshit that is holding you back from experiencing and living your Truth? What would be different if you were free from this bullshit?
- How is your relationship with your body? How do your general health, fitness level, and wellbeing serve your vision? How does your current physical condition help or hinder your ability to live your purpose? Have you had a thorough check-up from a doctor recently?

- What is your vision for your physical body one year from now? What about 10 or 20 years from now? How old do you want to live and how active do you want to be in your old age? Why?
- How would you describe your dietary habits, including what you eat, how much water you drink, and what else you consume or avoid consuming? What do you eat? How do you generally feel after eating? List some foods and eating habits that you would like to change. Be specific.
- Describe your level of physical activity. What is your relationship to physical exercise? What sort of physical activity do you enjoy doing? What kinds of physical activity would you enjoy more of if you were more physically fit?
- How is your sleep? And how do your sleeping habits affect your general state of wellbeing?
- What kinds of wellness practices have you experienced – yoga, massage, sauna, energy work, meditation, chiropractic, etc.? What did you experience? What sorts of wellness practices could you include in your life? What do you think the results would be?
- Do you have any addictions? If so, what are they and how do they affect your mind, body, and life? What would change in your life if you were free from these addictions?

Just like in the Mental Bullshit section, once you have identified and owned your Body Bullshit, what are you going to do about it? You may have tried to make changes and given up in the past. It can be different this time. You'll find that your Body Bullshit is actually tied up in your Mental Bullshit. All your limiting beliefs, conditioning, and programming is tied up with how you feel about yourself and how you show up in the world, including how you relate to your body. Once you start to get free from your Mental Bullshit, the Body Bullshit doesn't have the same weight. But, again, you'll need a plan. Start tackling one or two of the areas where you are the weakest. You can make small, incremental changes, but don't bullshit yourself by making changes that are so small that they aren't going to make a difference. Get help if you need it. Sometimes we just need to clean our gutters; sometimes we need a gut rehab.

LIFE BULLSHIT

Life Bullshit is the drama and chaos that comes from unconscious lifestyle choices. Money dramas, job dramas, and relationship dramas are the main forms of Life Bullshit that men need to pay attention to and to clean up. Again, we start with awareness and consciousness – we need to examine these different aspects of our life – and then we often have some leg work to do.

We will see tomorrow what we have broken and torn tonight, thrashing in the dark.

Jallaudin Rumi

We wake up in the same circumstances where we slept. Think about it: We don't wake up dressed, showered, wide awake behind the wheel of our car. We wake up in our cozy bed under our blankets. It's very common for men to get into this transformational work and 'wake up' in lots of messes. If we haven't been approaching our life in the most excellent way, we're bound to have some shit to clean up. These messes, however painful, can provide a kind of sick comfort for many men. Our friends, our habits, the places we hang out may very well be conspiring to keep us asleep. We need to look at all of this if we want to be properly awake.

Money Dramas

Money dramas can take many forms: tax issues, debts, out-of-control budgets, unpaid fines or bills, bankruptcies. Whatever the problems are, we need to attend to them or else they get worse. Money issues do not get resolved by being ignored. In fact, like issues with the body, money dramas just get worse and worse. Even if they're not blowing up in our faces, even if we think we are ignoring them, there is a part of us that knows the issues are brewing storms. Most men's sense of pride is deeply tied into their money. There can be a great deal of shame connected to financial problems. All I can say is: If you've got some money drama, handle it. Face it. Embrace the challenge and deal with it head-on or else it can suck up your energy, time, and joy, and cost you even more in the long run.

Some of us who didn't come from affluent backgrounds have a good deal of Mental Bullshit about money to get over. There are good training programs that you can get into to help rewire bad conditioning and undo limiting beliefs around money and prosperity. Money is our energy in a fixed form. It's important that we know how to wield its power. I'm not talking about becoming materialistic; I am talking about getting a handle on our bullshit factor with money. No one is more obsessed with money than a broke dad who needs to put food on the table. It's worth doing whatever you need to heal your bullshit about money, learn how to earn plenty of money and manage it well, and clean up any messes that your previous unconsciousness may have created.

Job Dramas

The dramas that come with a man's work life can come in all shapes and sizes and can weigh heavily on a man's psyche. Most men spend more time working than sleeping or doing anything else in their life. When dramas happen at work, they threaten a man's sense of pride and his livelihood too. Some men have jobs they love, but sometimes there's more job there than they can handle. Many men feel stuck in jobs that they are not connected to and that give them little or no joy. Other men make bad decisions and get into 'trouble' at work and get caught in that kind of chaos. For too many men, their job drama is that they have no work, or not enough work.

Whatever the job drama is, it sucks and can make us feel like our whole life sucks. This is especially true when we've given too much importance to our work.

Getting Free from Job Dramas

Whatever it is, the best medicine for a job drama is vision. If you find yourself in any of the above job dramas, or some other form of drama related to your work life, take about 20 steps back and find some time to do some visioning (see page 146). What is your vision for your work life? In your vision for life, what role does your work play? If you're in a job that doesn't match your vision, start planning an intelligent escape. Create a new vision for your work life that turns you on and get on track with it. In most cases, it doesn't fix anything right away, but this kind of offensive action can make your work drama suck a lot less and help you to manage this particular part of your bullshit so it's not on top of you. We need to have our work line up with our vision or else we either go crazy like a caged animal or we resign ourselves to being passive and half alive.

The other good medicine for most of the hard-working men I work with is a good dose of balance. Are you working so much that you're not giving yourself time to be with your loved ones or do the fun things you enjoy? 'All work and no play ...' – are you overdoing it at work and neglecting your physical needs for exercise, rest, good sex, and good nutrition? Many men's Body Bullshit stems from this aspect of their Life Bullshit. Clean it up. Design your work day around visits to the gym or chiropractor. Come up with a strategy to find good food options where you work. Little changes made with big awareness make big differences.

Relationship Dramas
Relationship dramas are complicated because they don't involve just you. They involve your friends and lovers and family members. It's important to examine all of your relationships and see what they're giving you and what they take from you. Ideally there is a symbiosis – it's a fancy word but a really good one. In a symbiotic relationship in nature, both animals or plants are benefitting – for example, birds eat a tree's fruit and benefit the tree by shitting out the seeds and helping the tree to reproduce. Ideally, the people in your life are benefitting you and you are benefitting them. Ideally there is a flow. Most dramas in healthy relationships happen when

this flow is interrupted and this balance is leaning too heavily to one side or the other. Then there are unhealthy relationships where there is no chance of symbiosis for whatever reason, or the work it would take to get to symbiosis is just not worth it. The most extreme unhealthy relationships are the ones we could call 'toxic.' Toxic relationships are the ones that are based on drama. There's little or no substance to the connection – people are just bringing out the worst in each other. It happens. But if you're really living your vision, you don't want to spend your time or energy on these no-win situations. Cut them loose.

Turkeys and Eagles
We want to be super clear about our vision of the kind of people we want in our life and our vision for the role we play in the lives of others. Many men on a transformational path run into trouble trying to relate to people who are wedded to their own bullshit. 'It's hard to soar like an eagle when you're surrounded by turkeys.' It's not easy, but sometimes we have to make hard decisions about the people we choose to give our energy to. Negative people in our life are serious liabilities. People who are stuck in their own bullshit will usually try to pull us down into theirs. Occasionally, rarely, once in a great while, our progress on the path will inspire one of the turkeys to get out of their bullshit and join us. Surround yourself with good people, people who are on a similar path themselves. Definitely make sure you surround yourself with good men. Strong backbones are contagious. Be fearless and relentless about cutting naysayers and toxic people out of your life. This includes family members. I believe we really have to choose our family. Assuming we are fulfilling what we truly believe is our duty to our children, siblings, parents, and extended kin, I really feel we owe it to ourselves to distance ourselves from anyone who pulls us back from being our best – even if it's our own blood.

I don't want to stroke your ego by saying this, but if you're reading this book and trying to walk a Red Road, you're an elite individual. It might not be easy to find lots of people who share your passion for excellence and transformation. The Red Road can be a lonely place. The Black Road is the more popular way, but we don't find our kindred spirits there. But you don't need a lot of 'soul people.' You just need a few. Having a handful of people that you can really be big around can give you the support and love and inspiration you need to stay on track and not feel like a freak. Being the lone wolf and staying by yourself all the time – if that's not what you want – is its own kind of relationship drama. It's important to have the right relationships and the right amount of company around you.

Spouses and Children
Many men have relationship drama with their spouses and children. There are whole books written about how to clean up these messes. All I will say here is: *clean them up*. It's worth it. Sometimes marriages have life-spans and it's time to let them go. But if you're staying with a spouse, walking this path means doing whatever it takes to make your marriage or committed relationship into something that is just as conscious and passionate and true. It's just like the rest of your vision. If you're sharing a bed with someone, you'd better make sure you're enjoying the same dreams at night. When we stay in intimate relationships with people who don't really know us, or in relationships that don't serve our greater mission and purpose, we're really asking for trouble. It sucks so much of our energy. On the other hand, when we have a conscious relationship, when we are on the same page as our intimate companion, that relationship can be a source of tremendous support. Our spouse or partner becomes our 'life partner.' We have each other's backs. We know each other's vision and we share

a common dream. When you have that, there's nothing like it. Of course there are fights and off moments – all relationships have those – but on the whole the partnership is about keeping each other on the Red Road.

If you are a father, your relationship with your kids is kind of a whole other category. You are your kids' father and you always will be. There's no other way to say this than to be blunt: Don't be a lousy dad. Don't beat them. Don't bail on them. Don't leak your unhappiness into them. It doesn't matter how difficult they are, or how busy you are, or how challenging your situation is. You are the elder in the situation, and you are the one on a path. Your good energy as their father is essential nourishment for their souls. Your negativity and unconsciousness is their soul's poison. Even if you're mediocre in every other area of your vision, do whatever you have to not to drop the ball on this one. Read books, go to counseling, talk to other dads, talk to your kids. Create a vision for yourself as a father.

Of course, nothing you do as a dad is insurance against drama happening with your kids. Kids are kids and they are learning to live life through the process of trial and error. No matter how excellent a Red Road father you become, you may still have upset, conflict, and drama with your kids. What keeps that drama from becoming Life Bullshit is your commitment to staying awake and applying yourself to staying on track with your purpose and living your vision.

As a dad, I know it's not easy. I really understand dads that bail on their families. I do. It's impossible to be the perfect dad. Parenting and breadwinning can make you feel like Sisyphus. In Greek mythology, Sisyphus was a deceitful king, whom the gods punished with a task: He had to roll an immense boulder up a massive hill, and then watch it roll back down again, and then roll it back up again – and watch it roll down again. Forever. As a dad we feel we're always making mistakes. As a breadwinner, it always feels like we could do better. It's just how it is. Create a vision for your fathering and do whatever you need to do to father from a place of bigness

> Whatever we do to be better dads, friends, partners, family members – it's worth it.

and wisdom and steady love. We will look more at fathering later in the book – for now, just make sure you are looking at and cleaning up any bullshit there.

Whatever we do to be better dads, friends, partners, family members – it's worth it. Your awareness and commitment to growth are the key ingredients that will clean up the majority of your relationship dramas.

Addiction

Addictions span all three kinds of bullshit and deserve a small section of their own. Addictions, if left unchecked, will ruin your body, mind, and life, and all but sink any aspirations you have for becoming deeply happy or truly powerful. The kind of addictions I'm talking about here can take the form of alcohol addiction, drug addiction (including weed), obsessive gambling, overeating, porn watching, compulsive shopping, or compulsive unhealthy sexual behavior. There are subtler addictions to substances like sugar and behaviors like watching TV, but for now let's just speak about the addictions that ruin lives quickly, drain bank accounts, get you locked up, and basically wreak havoc on your wellbeing.

If you're a full-blown addict, like a cocaine addict, obsessive gambler, or messy alcoholic, your whole life is full of bullshit on all levels. If you're a little less blatant, you can go a long time without causing much obvious chaos. Functional alcoholism and other varieties of low-level addictions are all too prevalent and easy to hide. Millions of men the world over are dulled and weakened by their evening cocktails or joints. If you have to have the drink after work, or you can't imagine not smoking your weed, you're addicted. It's not to say you're out of control or 'abusing' the substances, but if you think these mild addictions don't affect your parenting, your work performance, your health, or your future, you're wrong.

If you're a serious addict, then you are an expert at bullshitting yourself and others. Trust me – if there's one thing I know about, it's self-deception. You know what they say: You can't bullshit a bullshitter. So let me put it really straight: If you are an addict, get help.

Don't even bother finishing this book until you have a couple of months of 'clean time' – meaning time that you have totally abstained from your addictive behavior. Call someone now. Go to a meeting today. There are step-by-step programs for just about every kind of addiction imaginable, and they are all super useful. If in doubt, go to AA: they are the wise elders when it comes to addiction and they will be able to point you in the right direction. It might take some trial and error to find the right community and meetings for you, but don't wait. Get help, get clean and free from whatever addictive shit you're doing, then we'll talk. Doing the other Red Road work without handling this aspect of yourself is like putting lipstick on a pig. Don't waste your time.

If you're not sure, or you wonder about your drinking, or drug use, or other potentially addictive behavior, try abstaining and see what happens. It might be harder than you think. Anyway, it's a good thing to know about yourself. I require people in my advanced training programs to abstain from all drugs and alcohol for the duration of the training. This kind of total

> If you are an addict, get help.

sobriety is good for deep inner work, regardless of addictions. But if you find yourself needing to be a little high or a little buzzed to get through your life, you can take that as a good sign there's some bullshit to clean up somewhere.

BRUTAL HONESTY
- When you take a step back and look at your life, what stands out as the greatest example of bullshit that is distracting you from experiencing and living your Truth?
- How are your relationships?
- Are there any glaring relationship dramas that need your attention?
- What are some steps you can take to help lessen the dramas and enhance your relationships? Be specific.
- Make a list of people who are supportive of your purpose and vision, and people who are potential detractors.
- Do you have 'soul people'? If so, who are they, and how can you deepen your relationship with them?
- What is your ultimate vision for your main relationships?
- What is your ultimate vision for your social life in general?
- Describe your relationship with money. Do you have any active money dramas that need to be attended to? What about potential money

dramas? Is there anything that is brewing?
What do you need to do to take care of whatever
may be brewing?

- Are you well educated about money? Do you
know how to manage the money you have? What
are some ways you can train yourself when it
comes to money? What is your ultimate vision
when it comes to your material life?
- Do you love your work? If not, why?
- What could you do to make your work life more
in alignment with your greater vision?
- What is your ultimate vision for your
work life?

Once again, once you've identified your Life
Bullshit, it's time to get to work, brother. Out
of all the areas you have looked at, which one
would make the biggest impact if you took some
immediate action? Remember, the purpose of this
book is to help you to experience more radical
happiness. When you're facing down a chunk of
Life Bullshit, you've got a chance to transform
something that is helping you stay radically
unhappy. You don't have to tangle with all the
bullshit at once, but even one small change today
in one of those areas could start a chain reaction.
If you outlined some steps to reduce the drama
in your relationships, for example, then how are
you going to put those steps into action? Where
are you going to start? Remember there is a huge

difference between knowing what you need to do and actually finding the backbone to take action. It's a process. Just get clear on where you need to start and take one step towards it.

KEEPIN' THE DEVIL IN THE HOLE

No one gets totally free from all of their bullshit in one swipe. Part of being a man is learning to manage your bullshit and keep it in check. Getting free from your bullshit in the way the Third Key describes is about not being bound in it, not being caught in it or blinded by it. We each have our parcel of bullshit. A wise man knows how to insulate his purpose and vision from it. We need to learn to 'keep the devil in the hole.'

SUMMING IT UP

The Third Key – get free from your bullshit.
Your Bullshit –made up of all the ways you're not living your Truth.
Your Truth –what you believe to be the best way for you to think, speak, act, and live.
Innie – a man who keeps his bullshit quiet and under wraps.
Outie – a man whose bullshit is loud and obvious.
Humor – when dealing with your bullshit, it is important to have a sense of humor!
Progress not Perfection – the aim is not to get rid of your bullshit entirely. The aim is to make progress towards freedom from your bullshit.

Three Main Types of Bullshit:

Mental Bullshit: bad conditioning, limiting beliefs, triggers, and inner wounds. It is hard-wired and not just attitudinal.

Body Bullshit: whatever is unconscious, neglected in our body.

Life Bullshit: the drama and chaos that come from unconscious lifestyle choices.

As we progress through this book you will find that some of the inner stuff is deeper than others. The next chapter is going to take us into one of the deepest topics in men's transformation: how we relate as dads, fathers, and sons.

6

DADS, FATHERS, AND SONS

Every man has a dad. And with every father–son relationship there's a lot of room for growth. I'm not talking about improving your relationship with your dad. I'm talking about room to grow your relationship with yourself and your own manhood. This examination, looking deeply at our relationship with our father, is perhaps one of the most highly leveraged examinations a man can do on the path to finding his backbone.

To do it, we need to use brutal honesty and look at the ways our dad trained us – or failed to train us. You need to think about what kind of Mental Bullshit you're carrying around and the kind of Life Bullshit you're living in that comes from being the son of your father. We learn so much about ourselves and the way we relate to men and our own manhood by looking at our 'dad stuff.' Some men had great dads. Others had mean bastards for dads. Some men grew up with little fatherly input or no father around at all.

But for any boy, his dad is a huge icon. Our dads are our teachers, our male mentors, and, when we're little, our dad is nothing less than a god. Let's have a look.

DAD AS GOD

When we're babies, our parents are like gods. Their love, their attention, their care means everything to us. Without it, we literally won't survive. And if you've been around little babies you know they're all about energy. They are super tuned-in to the energy around them. Mom's feminine energy and dad's masculine energy leave a huge impact on us and affect how we later relate to masculine and feminine energy when we're adults. Our mother holds us and takes care of us, maybe she nurses us; through this connection with our mom we learn about feminine energy. It's obvious if you see a new baby with his mother – there is a profound energetic connection. While it might not be as obvious, the same thing happens with dad. He may hold us too, and his arms feel different to mom's: his arms are firmer, his touch has a different force to it. The time he spends with us is usually less. Dad smells different than mom. Dad's voice is different to mom's. Babies are tuned into all of this. They say that new babies recognize their dad's voice when they're born after hearing it from inside the womb. When Taryn was pregnant with our first son Jackson, I made a point to speak to him in his momma's belly every day.

So imagine yourself a small baby boy, crawling around, soaking in all the energy of your parents, of your home environment. What kind of energy did your dad put out? In a typical house, the mom sets the physical tone, and the dad sets the energetic tone. The mom usually oversees the food, the neatness or messiness, the decoration, the furniture. The father, on the other hand, is typically the one who fills the house with energy. Dad comes home, and a wave of his emotional, mental, and spiritual energy washes through the place. Make no mistake: You were definitely affected by that wave. This same phenomenon is true for homes where dad is absent. His very absence is his energy. Absence is a very powerful energy.

When I talk about our 'dad stuff,' don't misunderstand. I'm not talking about having 'daddy issues.' Dad stuff isn't something only some men have. We all have dad stuff – even if your dad was great, even if your dad wasn't there. In fact, I work with many men who lost their father early in their life, or whose father took off early on for whatever reason. Their 'dad stuff' is as strong – if not stronger – as it is for men who grew up with dad in the house.

Forget about your dad as a man for the moment. Remember, when you're really little, you don't know him as a fallible human. When you're a baby, your dad is a god. To you he was all powerful. How he was with you and around you wired you to relate to all men

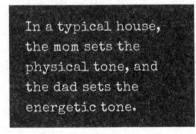

In a typical house, the mom sets the physical tone, and the dad sets the energetic tone.

and male energy in general. If he was harsh, or impatient, or cold with you, that had an effect on you. If dad was absent or abusive, this made a huge impact. Boys who are abused or abandoned by their dads – especially under the age of five – grow up with deep and toxic dad stuff to work out. When we're small like that the impact is deep because we don't yet have the ability to see dad's bullshit for what it was. When we are babies and our dad is a god, his actions make impressions in our psyche about all men, about male energy in general.

I'm not talking about what you think about your dad. I'm not asking you to evaluate his fathering or explore why your dad was the way he was. At this stage it doesn't really matter. When you were little – say under five – your little brain, nervous system, and deep psyche were getting wired and programed. Your conditioning was taking place. This part of our process is getting a handle on what kind of stuff might be brewing deep in your murky unconscious.

Every little boy wants his dad's love. He doesn't yet know that his dad is just a guy with all of life's challenges. So these early connections with our dad set us up to relate to men and masculine things. Some early connections turned us off men. Some early connections left us hungry for male attention. Some connections set us up to be naturally strong and masculine. Whatever your case, examine it and use it as fuel on your road to becoming the kind of man with backbone you want to be.

BRUTAL HONESTY

1. If you had to describe it, how would you describe your dad's energy wave? Can you sense what your own energy wave as a grown man is like? What kind of energy do you bring home? Can you learn anything by comparing these two?

2. How did your dad – as a god – behave around you?

3. When you were little, how did your dad treat you? What kind of energy did he emit? Was he a loving god? A harming one? A drunk one? An absent one? Did your dad yell with his loud male voice in the house? Did he slam doors? Was he drunk? Or high? Or depressed?

> Did he feed you? Was he a calming presence? Was he the 'stable one' in the home? Was he the one you ran to for safety, or was he the one you ran away and hid from? Examine these questions for yourself and you will get another window into yourself and your relationship with masculinity.

Your Mother's Version of Dad

Our mother tells us what a man is and our father shows us. The way that the goddess – mom – related to the god – dad – taught you in some way how you should relate to him, and thus how to relate to masculinity – and therefore how to relate to your own masculinity. That's how it works.

Few men grow up in a house with an honorable, strong, present, visionary father who is deeply respected by everybody. Most boys grow up with struggling, semi-present dads. Most of us grew up with dads who were – at least somewhat – at odds with mom. Some of us grew up in homes where dad was spoken of and treated with contempt. Some of us grew up with toxic or abusive dads

> Our mother tells us what a man is and our father shows us.

who deserved whatever contempt they got. The point here is that the way that our dad was regarded by the other people in the house – especially our mother – rubbed off on us. If your dad is seen as a doofus, or someone not to be trusted, or the one who has all the answers, this is going to have an effect on the way we expect men – and ourselves as men – to behave. This can show up as us going along with the template we were conditioned under, or show up as us being the total opposite.

MORE BRUTAL HONESTY

Who was your dad in the house? Was he the hero? Did your mother adore him? Or was he the asshole? Was he the bringer of joy and laughter? Or was he the sad-sack, tired, depleted worker? Was he the grinch? Was he an absence? Was he just a story? A shameful secret? Was he a clown? Who was he in your house? The answer to these questions will show you a ton about how you relate to male energy.

A Chip off the Old Block

Whatever ideas people had about your dad were surely projected on to you as well. When we are boys, we are always compared to our dad – especially by our mom. Everybody is watching us to see how we're like him or how we're not. Maybe they're hoping that we'll be more like him. Often they're hoping we'll be better. If our dad was a let-down to our mom or others, those people might look to us to make up for our dad's shortcomings.

This part of our conditioning and limiting-belief structure goes beyond just the opinions about our dad. We all grow up in environments where there's a predominating opinion about men in general. Sometimes it's out in the open, other times it's more undercover. Some boys are raised by man-wounded or man-hating mothers. Some of us were raised in homes where male was the 'enemy gender.' Others grew up in male-dominated households and inherited a sense of chauvinistic male entitlement.

My mom grew up with a dad who was a poor, abusive, violent, wife-beating, shotgun-toting drunk. She married my dad, who was a successful, gentle guy with no interest in brawling or hunting or anything very male. Her plan was to have a nice house with her gentle husband, maybe have a couple of little girls. And then she had four boys – four wild, pyromaniac, danger-prone boys! Our house was funny because we were all male except for her, but because of her and her dominant energy, there was clearly an anti-masculine energy in the house. All four of us turned out to be on the very masculine side of things. One of my brothers became a military pilot, another a bow-hunter. My oldest brother was a bounty hunter. And then there's me. It's almost like we had something to prove, or an inbred hunger for that masculine energy that she all but outlawed in the house.

There's no way to tell which way our environment is going to shape us as men. Sometimes we just fall in line and grow up to be like the other men in our family, or we become what the other people in our family expect us to become. Often we go the opposite way. An effeminate or gay boy raised in a male-loving, football-playing, military-man family might grow up to be extra effeminate. A boy raised in an

> We all grow up in environments where there's a predominating opinion about men in general.

all-female household, or in a house like mine where the dad is too soft or emasculated, might grow up to be extra masculine. It's just to say that there is an effect. You have to see what it is for you.

MORE BRUTAL HONESTY
Look back at the environment where you grew up.
How was your dad regarded? How was he treated?
Who was he in the house? How were men in general
regarded? How did the people in your house relate
to masculine energy? How has this affected you?

DAD AS TEACHER

As we grow past the infant stage where dad is a god, dad becomes our teacher. Some dads teach their boys how to fish or how to throw a ball. All dads teach us about being men, even if they're not trying to. Remember: Mom tells us what a man is, dad shows us.

Some dads do it directly: 'Son, a man will always open the door for a lady.' But this sort of direct teaching is the least of it. Most of the instruction comes just from being around him and watching him. He teaches us how to relate to work, how to relate to women, how to take care of our personal hygiene, and he teaches us what men do and what men don't do – mostly by example.

Whether he was aware of it or not, a big lesson that our dad taught us was about living our vision. He demonstrated this every day. By the time I was born, my dad, Carl, was already 44. From what I can gather, Carl had given up on his dreams years before. The Carl I knew wore suits, went to work, was the breadwinner for our family, stayed out of trouble, voted (Republican), raked the yard, drank martinis, watched TV, and grew old. He may have had a vision once upon a time, but over the course of his life, it seems that safety, security, and lack of conflict became his guiding lights. He was totally passive in the way he related to my mom and was generally depressed, drunk, defeated, and pessimistic. At least that's how I knew him. But I know he wasn't always like that.

When he was young he played music and raced sailboats. He was missing a kneecap. When I was little I was fascinated with his scar and the way one knee looked different from the other. The story goes that he had tried to jump over a fence holding a pitcher of beer at a pool party and didn't clear the fence. I learned from my older brothers that when my dad was young he had a passion for building things, and that he had an immaculate workshop

> All dads teach us about being men, even if they're not trying to.

with all of his tools, nails, and screws in their proper place. If you look at old pictures of him, he looked dapper, lively, tanned, well dressed – he was kind of a stud.

I knew nothing of this man. I never met that man who tried to jump the fence at the pool party. It's hard to even imagine him. In my time, my dad never had a boat. We belonged to the local yacht club, but all he ever did there was get drunk with my mother and her friends. We had a bunch of old musical instruments in the house. He played them badly a little bit when he had had too much to drink, but they were uncared for and out of tune. Our garage in my day was no immaculate workshop. It was a dusty, filthy, junk-storage space filled with rusty tools and old unused golf clubs and broken mowers. There was no order to the nails and screws. They were everywhere. I never saw my dad build much of anything.

I can remember him telling me in his fifties, 'The things you regret in life are not things you did, but the things you didn't do.' This was one of the only 'teachings' he gave me directly. A pretty good one, I must say. That, and the not so good, 'There's no use arguing with a woman, you will never win.'

Our dads teach us about vision. They teach us about honor. They teach us about a man's relationship to work and play and women and money. They teach us about sticking up for ourselves. We learn all this and more from dad – mostly by example.

My dad taught me many things about how not to be. Growing up around his defeated energy made something in me revolt and seek out a life that was the opposite in many ways. He also taught be how to change a car tire. That was pretty useful.

BRUTAL HONESTY
What did you learn from your dad? Take a minute and make a list.

- What did you learn from your dad about being a man?
- What did you learn about living with vision?
- What positive lessons did you learn?
- What negative lessons – in other words, how did you learn not to be?
- What valuable things did you learn from your dad?
- What things did you learn from him that you need to unlearn?

The last question above is an especially powerful one for us as men – what you need to unlearn about what your dad taught you. Your dad probably taught you many valuable things. But just as likely, he taught you a bunch of stuff that you need to unlearn. If you look at your limiting beliefs from Chapter 5, you'll see a few that came from him. If you look bravely at yourself as a man, you will see how the things he taught you are alive

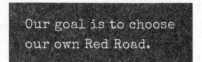

Our goal is to choose our own Red Road.

in you today. You'll find that you're very like him in some ways, and the opposite of him in other ways. No matter what, his influence is in you.

For us to be truly powerful and free, we need to find our own way and not live in reference to him. Whether we are living up to the model he taught us or living in rebellion against it, we are still basing our manhood on his manhood. Our goal is to be free. Our goal is to choose our own Red Road.

THE BEST DAD IN THE WORLD

Before we go looking at the dad stuff that comes from unfortunate connections with dads, let's talk about great dads. They do exist. There are bumps and rubs, even with the most outstanding fathers, but there are men out there who had dads that fathered from their bigness. Caring, loving, protecting, and successful dads for the most part create strong foundations for boys. But there can be 'dad stuff' to work out in those cases too. Some sons of great men have a 'shadow complex.' Deep down they feel they can never live up to their dad's awesomeness. Or there can be pressure from the outside. The son of the superdad is sometimes held to that super-standard.

No matter how good his training was, the son of a superdad needs to find his own way.

Assuming that the best dad in the world really did whatever he could to build up, encourage, and train his son, there is still sometimes work to do. No matter how good his training was, the son of a superdad needs to find his own way. Sons of great and loving dads often grow up holding onto a sense of wanting to please the superdad and keep his approval. We might even project this kind of stuff on our dads – we think that dad would disapprove of us taking a chance in life, or making some big change. And, not wanting to upset the 'best dad in the world,' we stay small to stay in his good graces.

Just look at it. Even if you have no 'issues' with your dad, examine that relationship and see how it informs your current-day manhood.

THE FATHER WOUND

Most sons didn't have the 'best father in the world.' Many of us had beaten, bored, or broken men for fathers. Some of us didn't have any father around at all. Most of us have at least one 'father wound.' And the father wound, more than just about any other inner wound, really affects our lives as men.

Sometimes father wounds can be subtle. We weren't encouraged or we didn't get as much love or attention as we wanted and needed as boys. Our dad didn't play catch with us, or come to our game. Often, father wounds can be much deeper. Some of us were outright harmed by our dads, beaten – even raped or assaulted – by our dads. Big or small, subtle or massive, we all have some kind of wound from our father. There is something innate in us that knows how great we are. If our dad doesn't live that greatness in his own life, or see and promote that greatness in us, there's a wound.

Kids need so much love. I see it with my own. If they had it their way, they would be with us every moment, soaking up attention and love. There's no way for any man to give his son as much love as the boy wants when he's little. I think it's actually impossible. So, if nothing else, that shortfall creates a wound. I really believe that, no matter how consciously I father my kids, I will still leave some kind of wound. I think it's inevitable.

Dads can be dangerous. Freud made a big deal out of what he called the Oedipus Complex. This is the idea that the mother and son are in a sort of conspiracy against the father and that there is a (sometimes murderous) rivalry between the father and son. There are plenty of places where you can learn about that. Let's just say that the relationships between fathers and sons are not always purely nurturing ones. There can be rivalries, there can be violence – active and passive aggression between dads and boys. Often fathers are not in touch with their hearts and are not fathering with any kind of vision. When this is the case, these men cannot really give the love and training that their son needs.

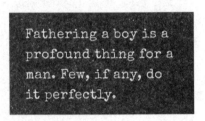

Fathering a boy is a profound thing for a man. Few, if any, do it perfectly.

In many cases, it's even more simple. Many of our dads needed to spend most of their time at work, away from their sons, and that distance did the wounding. Fathering a boy is a profound thing for a man. Few, if any, do it perfectly. Dads who are themselves not awake have almost zero chance of nurturing us in a wakeful manner. In some way or another, most of us were hurt by our dads, and our 'father wounds,' whatever they are, need to be dealt with and healed.

To young psyches, our father represents the primordial, powerful, protective energy of God. When he isn't protecting us, or he's acting from his weakness, our wiring gets all fucked up. There are two typical routes for the son of a wounding father.

Either he will grow up distrusting men and avoiding his own masculine energy. This is how we become soft guys, omega males, or man-hating, ironic, witty intellectuals. Or if he doesn't go that way, he will carry on his dad's negative legacy. Most wounding dads were raised by wounding dads. Men who are unhappy, unwell, and unloving usually learn that from their own unloving, unhappy dads. We don't want either of these outcomes. We are here to be big, awake, free, deeply happy, and truly powerful. Our father wound, when healed, can be like a doorway into our own mature, masculine energy.

Let's spend a little time looking at shaming dads, shrunken dads, absent dads, toxic dads, and dangerous dads.

Shaming Dads

A boy wants his father's approval so deeply. When this is denied, or when we're downright shamed or disapproved of by our fathers or other male mentors, our heart carries a profound wound. Shaming dads are the ones who are rarely satisfied. 'You're a disappointment' is the message they give us. This happens a lot with dads, even well-meaning ones. The baby boy gets more attention from his mom and dad gets jealous and bitter. Or the boy reminds the dad of something or someone he doesn't like. One man that I work with grew up with unhappily divorced parents. My client's face looks just like his mother's, so he grew up with his dad always saying nastily, 'You look like her and you act like her!' Sometimes it's the fact that the son reminds the dad of himself that he doesn't like. Every time the dad looks at the boy he sees something unpleasant in the 'mirror.'

If you are the son of a shaming dad, there's work you can do where you reclaim and reassert your general sense of worthiness and 'okay-ness.' If we grow up being seen through shaming, disapproving eyes, we will sometimes inherit those eyes and see ourselves with that same disapproving taint. It may sound corny, but one great practice is to give yourself a lot of praise. Praise yourself for everything you do right. Even little things like brushing your teeth or exercising. God knows you will curse yourself if you fail to pay a bill. Can't you also praise yourself when you do pay the bill?

PRACTICAL SUGGESTION

Try this: For the next 24-48 hours, try to abstain from self-criticism. When you do criticize yourself, notice if your dad's voice is in there somewhere. During the same time period, go over the top praising yourself for every good thing you do. It can be a private thing you do with your thoughts. It seems a little thing, but it has profound results.

Shrunken Dads

Shrunken dads leave another kind of wound. Shrunken dads are the dads who are beaten down, hen-pecked, or, for some other reason, shrunken as men. They wound us by being existentially lame, just as a powerful, happy father would feed us by being existentially robust. The shrunken dad starves his son. We grow up around his yielding, shrinking energy, and we can't help but get some of that shrunken energy in us. Sons of shrunken dads will tend to either be shrunken themselves or go to the other extreme and be super-sized, daredevils, or adrenalin addicts. That's what my brothers and I did. My dad was very shrunken, conservative, and overly safe, so we went to the other side. I got into drugs and punk rock and extreme lifestyles. Even after getting sober and into my self-development, I did it in a super-sized way. I traveled the world, got into extreme spirituality, learned to eat and cook exotic food, and still live a very alternative lifestyle.

Absent Dads

A father's energy is so important and powerful, and men's energies are so valuable and sought after, that one could argue that every son has an absent dad to some extent. Dad was at work. Dad was taking care of business outside of the house. Dad was at war. Dad was a traveling salesman. Dad was not there as much as our hungry little boy hearts would have liked.

Some dads were really gone. If your dad was actually absent from your life, that doesn't mean he wasn't there. He was there in his absence — his absence itself created your dad stuff. When there isn't a dad around, substitutes sometimes try to take up the slack. Step-dads, uncles, adopted fathers, etc. do what they can and often do great jobs. But there is a special spiritual connection between sons and their actual blood father. And when that man is not there, there is a vacuum that fills with all kinds of stuff. If you're lucky, it fills with strength and independence. If you're less lucky, it fills with demons.

Some dads are gone by chance. Some dads are killed by illnesses, accidents, wars, or crime. It's dangerous being a man, and some fathers exit the stage before they even get a chance to be our dads. This is hard for boys. It leaves that vacuum, which fills with who-knows-what, and it can create a lifelong beef with God or whatever you believe is the 'master of chance.' Boys

> Healing the absent-father wound can be a deep and long process.

who lose their fathers at a young age might grow up feeling cursed in some way.

Some other absent dads chose to not be there. At least that's what it feels like. There are the dads who commit suicide, or the dads that get locked up, or divorced dads that move away, or the dads who can't handle the family pressure and bail on their families. When our dads choose to leave us, for whatever reason, it feels personal. In a certain way it is. Somewhere inside we feel that we weren't important enough to keep them there. They chose a life of crime, they chose to kill themselves, they chose to become junkies and die – instead of choosing to be our dads. On top of the toll of not having our dad around, they also saddle us with the burden of feeling abandoned and rejected. That's a ton of shit to land on a little boy's psyche.

Healing the absent-father wound can be a deep and long process. What seems to help the men I've known who fall into this category is when they can find other sources of fathering energy. One of the men in our group lost his dad to suicide at a young age. He filled some of that void studying the written works of other great men. For him, the teachings of Plato, Socrates, and other great philosophers, and the lives of men like Ben Franklin and Abraham Lincoln have helped a great deal. He said once, 'I have about 20 fathers – and they're all dead.'

The other thing worth mentioning is that there are many examples – an extraordinary number – of famous men who lost their fathers at a young age. There's something about that intense pain and difficulty that sometimes forges greatness in men.

Toxic Dads

Some dads let their negativity go way beyond run-of-the-mill grumpiness, shaming, or disapproving. Some dads are so dark or unloving, so critical or unhappy, that they become poisonous to their sons. Growing up with a toxic dad can harm a boy and create a self-hatred and inferiority complex that can truly ruin a man's life. These kinds of dads shit on your vision and stamp out your natural free, wild power.

Toxic dads can take the form of depressed fathers or fathers with addictions. Not the drunk-driving, door-kicking, shouting, dangerous addict dads, but the functional-alcoholic dads, the dads who are able to maintain their addictions and keep their jobs. Toxic dads can also be failure dads. They've failed in business, or in love, or in life, and they live from that place of failure, leaking that 'born to lose' energy all over their sons. They may feel competitive with their son and want to keep their son small to keep themselves from feeling little. The unhappiness of the toxic father is contagious.

The dysfunction and misery of the toxic dad isn't the outer kind of dysfunction and chaos that creates bruises on skin. It's an inner thing. The toxic dad puts a poisonous energy in the atmosphere that pollutes. When he hates his life, or hates your mother, or resents his kids, that funk comes out of him and gets absorbed. Of course, if you had a toxic dad, you weren't the only one affected. Your mom too went into whatever her dance was to cope and compensate for toxic dad's nastiness.

There are some really powerful ways to detox our toxic-dad stuff. They're not so different from the way you detox your body. First you stop taking in the toxins. If your toxic dad is still alive and still toxic, take a break from him. I know adult men who still take shit from their toxic dads. If that's you, take a break. You don't have to disown him, but to get free from the inner poison you do need to do this step. Once you've gotten some space, or if he's passed away or not around, make some effort to eliminate the toxic residue you carry. It might be in the form of his stuff – physical heirlooms or possessions you've inherited. It might be in the way you behave, or the way you speak. It might just be the pain and poisonous energy you still carry in your own belly.

What do you have today that reminds you of his toxic energy? Do you have some of the same habits? Do you catch yourself saying (out loud or in your head) the nasty things he said? Notice how you talk to yourself when you've made an error, even a stupid little one. Chances are, you'll hear the toxic dad's voice. Take a break from that kind of talk and be vigilant about letting it creep back in.

Then flush your system with good dad energy. Find examples of strong men that you admire and flood yourself with their energy. You may know such men personally – if so, bring them close and spend time with them. Or they may be authors or artists or spiritual masters that you admire. Get their energy into that part of your heart where your toxic dad's venom lived. Do whatever you need to do to give yourself a nurturing, life-affirming experience of

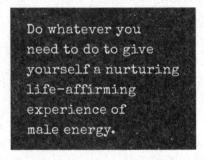

Do whatever you need to do to give yourself a nurturing life-affirming experience of male energy.

male energy. It's especially good if you can get it from older men, or men who are powerful in some way.

Deep meditation is a good practice for clearing out that 'deep belly poison.' When you go inside and use your breath to clear away those old energy patterns, it's like throwing open windows and doors in a house and letting the fresh air in. Find a master teacher to learn from or look up our meditation courses and retreats.

The main thing is that you recognize that whatever that toxic shit is, it's his – not yours. If you grew up with a toxic dad, it's because your dad didn't do this backbone work you're doing now.

That's not your fault, or your problem. You don't have to carry his unhappy bullshit.

Dangerous Dads

Dangerous dads are the abusers. These are the dads who are so out of control that they completely violate the protective principle of the father–child relationship. When our fathers harm us, beat us, molest us, endanger us, or expose us to violence, they create a very deep father wound. Many men who have this in their past need to seek out specific support to help them to get some of that in order. There is no shame in seeing a good therapist to sort out the deeply held trauma that dangerous dads can inflict. There are some great therapists out there – there are many god-awful ones too. If you can find one that understands your vision for life and is wanting to help you get there, it can be well worth the time and money.

Every Other Kind of Dad

I fully understand that your dad may not fit neatly into any of these categories. Most of our dads were mixed, to say the least. Unless our dads really had their shit together, chances are we have some baggage to deal with in the dad department. I will leave it to you to look at your dad and who he was, and to figure out what you need to do to be your own man.

LEARN TO FATHER YOURSELF

I will share with you some best practices for sorting out your dad stuff at the end of this chapter. For now, let me just say that it all comes down to learning to be your own father. You couldn't do it then. But you can now. You can imagine that the little you – whatever they called you back then – is still an active part of your present-day psyche. He's in there, and he needs the big adult you to be that wise and loving protector. This is one of the biggest benefits of doing this work. As you learn to live in your bigness, and live with a real, mature, masculine backbone, you can give shelter to your smaller parts. You can give that good father energy to the hungry parts that need it. You can give yourself counsel, you can forgive your own mistakes, you can encourage yourself to rise above your own fears. You can be that great Red Road father to yourself. You have to be that father to yourself.

When you make this shift, when you've healed the main part of your father wound and you've started really fathering yourself, then your relationship to your actual father can evolve, no matter how he was as a dad.

CUT HIM SOME SLACK

As we come into our own fatherhood, whether we have our own kids or not, we will learn to appreciate where our 'old man' was coming from. I don't mean excusing or condoning abuse or neglect or the other unconscious, unloving things our dad may have done. I'm talking about being in a place of true bigness that allows us to have some compassion and empathy for him. It's not easy being a powerful man. If you have kids, you know: it's impossible to be a perfect father. We will go deeper into all this in the chapter on the King Power, but, for now, let's just hold the vision that we can forgive our dad if he needs forgiving. Not to let him off, but to free ourselves from the burden of resentment and heaviness, and any other Mental Bullshit we may be carrying as a result of that heaviness. If our dad was amazing, let's hold the vision that we can let ourselves off the hook about living up to his legend.

No matter what he was or who he is, remember the Three Keys: your purpose and vision is not served by having unresolved bullshit lingering in your heart or in your head. Making peace with your dad – whatever that takes – is a very fundamental thing to do. When we free ourselves from our dad stuff, our energy is freed up to follow our vision and live from our place of bigness, with our backbone fully intact.

SUMMING IT UP

Dad as a God – when we're children, we often see our dad as a god.
Dad Stuff – all men have dad stuff. Even if your dad wasn't there, you still have dad stuff.
Your Mother's Version of Dad – the way that your mom related to your dad taught you how you should relate to him.
A Chip off the Old Block – whatever ideas people had about your dad were surely projected on to you as well. Boys are always compared to their dads, especially by their moms.
Dad as Teacher – mom tells us what a man is, dad shows us. Our dads teach us about vision. They teach us about honor. They teach us about a man's relationship to work and play and women and money. They teach us about sticking up for ourselves. We learn all this and more from dad – mostly by example.
The Father Wound – many men have beaten, bored, and broken men for fathers, or no father around at all. Most of us have at least one 'father wound,' even if we had the best dad in the world.

DAD'S STORY

Write a short biography of your dad. Don't call him 'dad.' Call him by the name that people called him. I find doing this really helps us to see our dads as men, rather than as the daddy-gods that they were to us when we were little.

See if you can find a picture of your dad from back then. Get one when he was the age he was when you were little. Examine the picture and try to get yourself 'into his shoes' and imagine where he was coming from as a man, what challenges he was facing, what the motivations were for his actions or non-actions. This can be very intense. Don't do this in a half-assed way, and don't be afraid of any feelings that might come up. Feel them, note them, don't judge or suppress them.

Investigate: What were the biggest mistakes your dad made as a man? What can you learn from these mistakes? What steps can you take to avoid making the same mistakes in your life?

Try to learn about your dad's relationship with his dad. If your dad is alive you can interview him and mine him for info. Like it or not, you are part of a continuing tradition.

Getting to know something about that tradition can be very useful as you walk your path.

Take your 'inner boy' for 'play-dates.' Make time to nurture that part of you that didn't get nurtured by your dad. Practice being that big, strong, wise father to your own young heart. You don't have to tell anyone what you're doing. Just do it. Ride go-carts, eat ice cream, go to the museum – whatever. Follow that free, fun-loving part of your heart. Sometimes we do this automatically as we father our own kids, but this practice is a little different. Go alone and make it just for you.

Now that we have looked closely at the Three Keys to Happiness and how they apply to your life, in the next section we are going to go deeper and start putting the keys into action in your life.

Part Two
THE FOUR SIDES OF THE COMPLETE MAN

Earlier I introduced the Lakota idea of the wica, or complete man. As you get to know yourself and you start getting the Three Keys, it is crucial that you have some framework to help you craft a new vision for yourself as a complete man. Having backbone doesn't just mean being strong, or having integrity, or being clear, or being kind. The wica is fierce when he needs to be and is gentle when tenderness is required. He can take care of his business in the most excellent way when it's time to work, and then open himself to the finest pleasures in life when it's time to play.

In this next section, I will introduce a time-honored framework — one that I have used myself and one that I have used with countless men to help them to flesh out a new kind of bigness as a man.

I'll share with you the core masculine energies or archetypes of the King, the Warrior, the Mystic, and the Lover. These are four essential energies that every man needs to learn how to own and operate to really be a man with solid backbone.

7

THE FOUR POWERS

It's pretty easy to figure out what kind of man you don't want to be. But to make real progress on our path, it's important to focus on what kind of man we do want to be.

In this chapter, I'm going to introduce you to the four main powers that every conscious man has to own deeply and operate well. They are: the King, the Warrior, the Mystic, and the Lover. These four primordial male energies – or flavors of male energy – are hard-wired powers in men. In the typical modern, disempowered man, they are mostly unknown, unclaimed, or under-used. For us to be deeply happy and truly powerful in our life, they should all be conscious, intact, strong, and balanced. You can think of them as four legs of a table, or four different gears that you operate from. As men, we aren't just one thing. We are complex, and this model helps us to live into that complexity in a powerful, masculine way. The great thing about working with these energies is that they are universal. No matter what kind of man you are, or what culture you come from, you will have these four facets. They might look completely different in each man; nonetheless, they are there – either owned or disowned, strong or weak. Over the years, I have gained so much from looking at myself through the lens of these Four Powers. Let's take a look.

THE KING

Our King Power is our inner sense of authority over ourselves and the world we choose to create. The King is the power in us that is responsible for creating a vision for our life and then making sure that we stay on track with the vision. The King is all about the 'big picture.' The King decides what is important in our life and what is not. It's our power to make big decisions. The King energy brings order to the Kingdom, and when there is no King on the 'throne,' chaos rules the day. In our case the King energy is responsible for holding and caring for the various aspects of our life as men and making sure they are all moving forward and in alignment with our purpose. A man without a King is like a driver asleep at the wheel.

The King is the chief of the tribe, he is the father of the family, he is the commander of the troops, the commander of our lives. The work I do with men to get the First Key – know your true purpose in life and be on track with your vision – is getting them into their King Power. In the Indian tradition, there's a great Sanskrit word for King energy – *ishwaria* – which translates loosely into the English word 'lordship.' When we have ishwaria, we are the masters of our world, not in the sense of dominating anyone, or being a dictator, but in the

> The King isn't about ruling his Kingdom – he is about taking care of his Kingdom.

sense that we are in control of ourselves. When we have this quality, we are awake and aware of what's happening in our life, and we are empowered, ready to serve the world around us. This is an important point: The King isn't about ruling his Kingdom – he is about taking care of his Kingdom. A good King cares for his Kingdom and provides whatever it needs. Forget kings in the movies and on TV. The King Power we're talking about here is the part of us that makes our life awesome and makes sure that everything in our life is flourishing and taken care of. The King takes responsibility. The King cannot pass the buck. Having our King Power intact isn't an ego thing, it's an example of genuine power. The King Power says to us, 'I'll take care of it. I've got this. Keep your eyes on the goal. Don't worry.'

As I said, this power is hard-wired in every man, but few men really live with their sovereign King Power. Most men give their King away. They give their authority over to their wife, to their boss, to their competition, to their 'duty,' to their life problems, to their government. Men who lack their King will even give their power to their kids. It really doesn't matter. If a man doesn't have his King, or has a weak King, his power is really up for grabs. When we've forgotten our King, we're often bitching and moaning and feeling like victims. If a man without a King has a problem, he approaches it by whining or complaining. 'Shit happens' is the mantra of the man with no King. A man in possession of his King chooses his life circumstances. If a man with a strong King has a problem, he takes charge and handles it. His life is his – his body, his mind, and his destiny are his.

We will learn more about how to work with our King Power, but first we need to look at how the King is balanced by the Warrior, Lover, and Mystic Powers.

THE WARRIOR

The Warrior Power is one of the most essential powers for today's man to cultivate. The Warrior Power is the 'get it done' energy of a man. The Warrior serves the King by protecting his authority and doing the foot work to make his mission happen. The King makes decisions, the Warrior enforces the decisions. The Warrior energy is the skill we use to fight the battles that need to be fought. It's the energy we use to muscle through the hard aspects of life. The Warrior Power is our grit. A man without his Warrior Power is a pushover, a doormat, a coward.

The Warrior is the combat soldier, the temple guard, the tireless worker, the fearless one who comes to the rescue. The Warrior is the defender of what is weaker and needs to be defended, and the defender of our vision for life. He's not about fighting all the time; the Warrior is not about acting tough. The Warrior is a master of his energy and doesn't waste it with showing off. The Warrior Power is what we summon when we need to take a stand. It's the part of us that says 'Enough!' to the bullshit in our life. The Warrior doesn't take shit from anybody. The Warrior is our power to 'go for it,' seize the day, and get stuff done. The Warrior is our fearlessness and our ability to withstand pain. Our Warrior Power says to us, 'Less talk, more action! Stand up! Don't quit! You can do it! You can take it! No fear! Fuck the naysayers! Here we go!'

> The Warrior is our power to 'go for it,' seize the day, and get stuff done.

Every man has a Warrior Power, but few men really use it. When we're out of touch with our inner Warrior, we're floppy, passive, easily swindled, easily distracted, and easily defeated. Our dreams are just dreams. We've got no teeth. Our King Power has no army to make his vision happen, or defend it against doubt and hardship. Without a strong Warrior, the King is all talk, nothing more than a politician. Men without a strong inner Warrior don't relate well to other men and tend to surround themselves with women – and are usually dominated by the women they're intimate with. When we forget our Warrior Power, we tend to live in our heads, or hang out in virtual worlds where our salt is never tested. We sit on the couch and fight fearsome video game battles, and then surrender without a fight to the Doritos and beer. A spiritual guy might perform the 'warrior pose' in his yoga class but lack the ability to stand up for himself in life. Without our Warrior Power, we lack thump.

The King and the Warrior are two of the most essential powers for us to cultivate, but without the Mystic and the Lover, we'll be way out of balance.

THE MYSTIC

The Mystic Power is a man's power of wisdom, his intuition, and his ability to connect to Spirit and bring that spiritual energy into his material world. The Mystic is the King's advisor. He is the balancer to the King. While the King is holding court, and the Warrior's taking care of business, the Mystic is in his chambers, meditating on the mysteries of the universe, or whispering advice into the King's ear. Without the Mystic advising him, the King can get caught in his bullshit. Mad Kings hang their advisors. Our Mystic Power is our power to transform ourselves on the inside. It's the power that we cultivate so that we're not the slaves of our chattering mind. On the simplest level, the Mystic is our power of learning and wisdom. Men without their Mystic Power intact are doofuses: they're cavemen – insensitive, reactionary, typical, and stupid.

The Mystic Power is not a religious thing. Institutional religion is the substitute for true mystical experience. A Mystic is not concerned with the definitions and rules that

> Our Mystic Power is our power to transform ourselves on the inside.

religions are obsessed with. The Mystic doesn't need the formalities of doctrine; the Mystic is intimate with the Great Mystery. When our Mystic Power is strong, Spirit is an experience, not just an idea. When I help a man to get the Second Key – cultivate a deep and authentic spiritual connection – I'm helping him to make space for his Mystic Power. The Mystic is the sorcerer, the prophet, the true yogi, the wise man, the shaman. The Mystic is the 'seer.' Our inner Mystic gives us the ability to see beyond the obvious. When our Mystic Power is strong, we're able to live a life guided by wisdom and empowered by Spirit. We're able to transform ourselves. This is the real power of the Mystic – the power to transform our consciousness. The Mystic knows that transformation is an 'inside job.' If we are to be deeply happy and truly powerful, we have to learn to look inside, work on ourselves, and be able to adopt alternative ways of thinking and seeing. When this power is weak or absent, then we're stuck being whoever we are. Our inner Mystic is unafraid of introspection and learning something new.

Like the King and the Warrior, every man has an innate Mystic Power, but this power is disowned by most men. Some men are very intellectual, but have little or no ability to think or feel spiritually; they've shut off their power of intuition. Plenty of men consider anything spiritual to be 'woo-woo' or 'kumbaya.' For many years I have taught meditation and this inner Mystic work to military veterans. I have noticed a big difference in the reactions of 'regular' foot soldiers and those of elite military operators and people from Special Forces. The regulars are standoffish at the idea of cultivating a spiritual practice; they have to be sold on the idea. The elite operators, on the other hand, jump at the chance to learn ways to hone their intuition and mystical skills. In ancient times, men would strive to cultivate wisdom. Wise men were sought out and greatly respected. This notion is all but lost today. Guys, dumb jocks, and hard men seem almost to take pride in being dense and stupid. I will give you some powerful, simple practices to enhance your Mystic Power. For now, let's just say that we need it.

THE LOVER

The Lover Power is the power of enjoyment. It's the part of us that can embrace beauty and pleasure. It's also our ability to create beauty and give pleasure. The softness and openness of the Lover energy balances the hardness of the Warrior. When the King finishes his ruling for the day and the Warrior finishes his battle, when the Mystic has done his prayers and meditations, they all retire to enjoy their favorite pleasure. The Lover is the King's ability to enjoy his wealth and promote the beautiful things in his Kingdom. It's the Warrior's ability to take off his armor, lie down, and have his wounds tended to by gentle hands. Our Lover energy is the part of us that opens up and says 'Yes!' to new experiences. It is our 'soft side' that has to be there to nurture our children and open our hearts to loving and being loved. Love is an essential nutrient for every human spirit. Too many men are stuck and cut off from love. Men need to have this part intact to avoid becoming dry, miserable, and grumpy sons of bitches.

> The Lover Power in a man is also his masculine sense of beauty.

The Lover is the Romeo, the artist, the gourmet, the sexual connoisseur, the nature lover. He is the one with giant sensual arms that can wrap around anything. The Lover energy isn't exactly hedonistic, it has limits – especially when it is balanced by the King's sense of purpose and the Warrior's discipline. But the Lover Power basically wants to merge with and enjoy everything. It is a dog having its belly scratched. You experience the Lover when you climb into a bath of hot water and feel your physical tension release. We connect with the Lover energy when we're having good sex. Notice I said good sex, not just humping or beating off. If we can get out of our heads and really let go into the experience, the sexual moment is a peak experience of the Lover energy. 'Let go and experience' is the mantra of the Lover.

The Lover Power in a man is also his masculine sense of beauty. A man will get in touch with his Lover energy when he's feeling the leather seats of a fine car, or admiring the craftsmanship of handmade wooden furniture. It's in our sense of grooming and clothes. Our inner Lover enjoys fine colognes and perfumes, fine whisky and women. Our Lover Power thrives in natural beauty and craves being in fresh air and the splendor of the wilderness.

When a man has denied his Lover energy, he will become joyless and harsh. The Lover gets lost in a typical 'working man's' sense of self-sacrifice and self-denial. If we've made big mistakes in life or think of ourselves as failures, we might lock up our inner Lover as a form of self-punishment, as if we don't deserve to enjoy the pleasures of life. Some men have religious baggage about their Lover: it's sinful to experience too much pleasure, even if the pleasure itself isn't sinful. Workaholics need more Lover, and so do hard macho men and men suffering from depression. We will have a whole chapter about the Lover to go deeper into this, but for now, just understand that it's an important piece of the whole-man puzzle.

The Lover balances the Warrior that serves the King, who is advised by the Mystic. When there's not enough Mystic, we become stupid, we're cut off from our deep wisdom and spiritual side. If we lack Lover energy, we don't enjoy life, we become too hard. If we lack Warrior Power, we can't get done what we need to get done. And if we lack King energy, we lose our vision and our life is not really even ours to live.

All four of these powers need to be intact and in balance.

Men tend to favor one or two of the powers and be weak in the others. You might have a strong Warrior nature, but you lack King, so you put all of that Warrior energy into a job that you don't even care about. Or you might be a Mystic Lover and love to party and have great intuitive abilities and compassion, but you lack grit and the ability to take care of others.

In the following chapters, I am going to share indepth knowledge about the Four Powers and also give you some best practices for enhancing each one. First, it's time for some more brutal honesty.

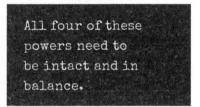

All four of these powers need to be intact and in balance.

SUMMING IT UP

The King – our inner sense of authority over ourselves and the world we choose to create.

The Warrior – the 'get it done,' hunter-killer energy of a man.

The Mystic – a man's intelligence and wisdom, his intuition, and his ability to connect to Spirit and bring that spiritual energy into his material world.

The Lover – the power of enjoyment, of loving and being loved.

BRUTAL HONESTY

Be quiet and sit down with your journal or notebook. Take a minute to go through these questions and write down the answers. Don't worry about getting them 'right' – get 'em true.

- If you look at yourself and your Four Powers honestly, what do you see?
- Which power or powers are strongest for you? Which are weakest?
- Why are your strong ones stronger and your weak ones weaker?
- What is the price you pay in life for lacking strength in the weaker powers?
- What advantages in life do you enjoy when you're able to live through your stronger powers?

VISION

Close your eyes and take time to see yourself living life with *all Four Powers* totally intact. See your Warrior, King, Mystic, and Lover energies as you understand them now, full-on and running strong. How does it feel?

BRUTAL HONESTY

How would you be different if you had these Four Powers intact? What would change in your life?

We've highlighted the Four Powers available to you as a man. In the next four chapters we will go deeper into these powers so you can start to experience more of them in your life.

8

THE KING

Of all of the powers, this is the most important one for a man to get a hold of. Plainly put – if you have your King Power intact, you are in charge of your life. If you don't have it, you're not in charge of your life. And if you're not in charge, all kinds of bullshit can take over. Your life becomes a kingdom with no ruler. You're basically fucked. In this chapter, we are going to help you zero in on this basic masculine power and get yours awake and in his seat.

BACK TO PURPOSE AND VISION

On the Red Road, you need to know what is at the center of your life. What does your life revolve around? When your King is in his seat, your work, your relationships, your money, your recreation, your health, and everything else all arrange themselves around the centerpiece of your purpose and vision. The job of your

King Power is to be clear on that purpose and vision, and then make sure it stays in the center and that other things don't overtake that position.

> Your King is the one who keeps your true purpose and vision in the middle, like the hub of a wheel.

When men are out of touch with their King, they allow their work to be the centerpiece. Younger men will often put their relationship or their entertainment in the center. If we get ill and don't have our King, our body and its crisis becomes the center. Loud bullshit like money trouble, divorce, and work disasters will push their way into the center if the King loses his seat for a minute.

Man, if you get this point, your life will change. Your King is the one who keeps your true purpose and vision in the middle, like the hub of a wheel. Then you always know what your next right action is – or at least your next right direction. This is the path to deep happiness and True Power.

If you don't know your purpose, if you don't know what's supposed to be in the center, there is no limit to the number of things that will make their way in there.

If your King Power is intact and in balance, you will hold the key to: your true purpose, your Core Values and honor code, your backbone, your vision, and your role as Father of your Kingdom.

1. TRUE PURPOSE

Finding your Purpose
Sometimes we just look within and know our purpose. Sometimes we choose our purpose. Sometimes we hear a calling and know

our purpose that way. Let me share my purpose with you to make this a little more clear.

My purpose: To be a servant of God's love and human transformation. To be an excellent, loving soul-father.

Just putting that here sends a bolt of energy down my backbone. Understand: This purpose has been honed, and meditated on, and worked with for more than 25 years. Every word in it is intentional.

The first sentence has been my purpose since I was about 19. The second sentence is more recent; I added it after having my first son. I think it'll help you with yours if I explain how both parts came about. I came upon the first part watching a film about Mother Teresa. At college, a teacher had us watch it for a class called Mystical Consciousness East and West. In the movie, there was a scene where Mother Teresa was rescuing some disabled kids who were trapped in a hospital in war-torn Beirut. The scene was horrific and heroic at the same time. Mother Teresa and her nuns swooped in to this bombed-out hospital, picking up the terrified children with so much love. There was rubble and screaming and suffering everywhere, but the nuns were totally unscathed by it. They were just taking care of business. Their commitment was total and Mother Teresa was unstoppable. In one shot, Mother Teresa picked up an emaciated, trembling boy and beamed a smile into his eyes and said, 'BEAUTIFUL child!' The boy's shaking subsided. Watching all this on the screen, I heard my 'calling.' I knew that was what I wanted to do: I wanted be a servant of love the way Mother Teresa was. After I heard that vocation, that calling, I couldn't imagine doing anything else with my life. I was an art student at the time and was a part-time dabbler in spirituality. After hearing this call, I started taking more classes in humanities, went much deeper in my spiritual training, and got a job working as a youth counselor. Eventually I changed my major and decided to do art as a hobby and find a career where I could help people more directly.

I was lucky; I didn't write my purpose down or even speak it to anyone. I don't think I even put it into words until years later. I didn't need to write it down because it was so strong and so clear in my heart. From then it was – and continues to be – the guiding light for all of my life choices. It was that guiding light that sent me to India and led me to become a teacher, and ultimately it was the light that guided me to write this book. Since that day, whatever means I chose, the end was to be a servant of God's love and human transformation. I have been a trainee, a trainer, a writer, a teacher, a healer, a project manager, but everything I've done has been a means to that end – to be a servant of God's love.

When Taryn was pregnant with our first son, Jackson, I heard the second part of the call. To be an excellent, loving soul-father. The prospect of being a dad was huge, but it also put me in touch with a deep nurturing masculine part of myself that wasn't just about paying the bills or changing the diapers – it was about holding that big protective fathering space for my kids' souls, for the soul of whatever I'm fathering. So whether it is with my family or with the students that study with me, or within my community, this soul-father energy is part of my purpose.

Three Important Ingredients
For the purpose to be strong, it needs to come from your heart, be specific, and be unconditional.

Come from your heart means that it has to be really authentic to you. It's not necessarily what your boss, your wife, your religion, or your society wants your purpose to be. It's up to you to dig deep and get a true purpose that you feel passionate about. Both halves of my purpose 'came to me' as undeniable truths that I had to live, but often there is no 'calling' as such. You might have to dig in and really listen to your heart and try out different paths to uncover your deep purpose.

Specific means that you really choose every word of your purpose. I could write a paragraph about each word in mine and explain why it's there. Specific also means not too universal. In my purpose, I added 'and human transformation,' because just 'a servant of God's love' was a little too vague for me. Over the years I have gotten clearer on how I am meant to serve that high principle of 'God's love' – the main way I do it is by facilitating human transformation.

Unconditional means that your purpose is your purpose, no matter what. It so happens that my career as an author and transformational teacher as it is today totally fits my purpose. But, as I mentioned before, this purpose has been executed in many different ways over the years. My purpose would still be my purpose, even if I could no longer do this work. It would be my purpose if I worked at a supermarket or was locked up in prison, or was in a catastrophe: the building's on fire; I'm serving God's love. My purpose is to be an excellent and loving soul-father even if – heaven forbid – I were to lose my kids. I will be a soul-father to my life, to my world. It is what I am. Following this purpose is what keeps my King in his seat.

Ends and Means
If you want to keep your purpose as the centerpiece of your life, you have to know how to separate 'ends' from 'means to ends.' My purpose happens to be heavily career related. This is common for men. But my work is not my purpose, it's a means for me to fulfill my purpose. If I weren't careful, my work – and all of the dramas

that go along with it – would easily become my centerpiece, the thing that everything else revolves around. I have to stay alert and remember what my actual purpose is and understand my work is a powerful way to live my purpose.

Always Know your Place

When you know your purpose, you know your place. It doesn't have to be something high and mighty; it just needs to be deeply true to you. A good friend, who is a chef and life-long restaurateur, says, 'No matter what happens – a death, a disaster, a war breaks out – I know where I'll be: in the kitchen, feeding people.' When 9/11 hit he was at his restaurant in Lower Manhattan. While everyone was freaking out, he was firing up his BBQ. He knew his place. The King was on his throne, making food, feeding people.

```
             YOUR PURPOSE

    Take a moment to sit quietly with your
    journal or notebook and take a stab at
    writing your true purpose. Just try and
    see what you come up with. Make sure it
    comes from your heart, and is specific and
    unconditional. At first let it be really rough
    or vague. Afterward you can go back and hone
    it and choose every word carefully. Remember,
    if you really can't think of a purpose, your
    purpose is totally clear: Your purpose is to
    get clear about your purpose!
```

MORE BRUTAL HONESTY

When you've put your true purpose into words, look at your actual life and see how much you live your purpose. Is your purpose the center of your life? Assuming your deep purpose isn't always at the center, what takes its place when it's absent? What's the Black Road center of your life? How does this affect you and your life?

What would need to change in the way you live for you to really be living your true purpose? If you made those changes, how would your experience of life be different?

Once you know what your purpose is, if you want to 'get your King,' you need to start creating a vision. The Red Road is the road of living your vision.

2. CORE VALUES AND HONOR CODE

We are going to take you through a process of creating a vision for your life, but before we can do that, you need to get super clear on who you are as a man and who you want to be. Your vision isn't just a 'what' thing, it's a 'how' thing too. There are only so many outside circumstances that we can control. What we can control – or, better yet, command – is our own inner being. We can be in command of the way we are. A man with his King Power intact knows himself in this deep way.

For centuries, men have had a sense of honor, a sense of what makes a man good, trustworthy, and respectable: a sense of Core

Values. Most men these days rarely think about honor, or what it means to be a good man. This is what we think of when we talk about men who lack backbone. Men may tell themselves, 'Come on, man up, be better, grow a backbone, stop being a pussy!' But these are just jabs with no substance, if we don't have intelligent alternatives. When you know what your Core Values are, when you have an honor code, you know how to correct yourself. You know the direction to better yourself. When you live according to your Core Values and really follow your honor code, you have a sense of power and healthy pride. This is a crucial part of the King work. Men who have power, but no sense of values, become tyrants. Like your true purpose, your honor code serves as an inner compass to let you know when you're on track or off track. Your honor code is not about what you're able to accomplish in life, but rather the way you conduct yourself and the spirit that you live your life in.

In our men's weekends, we like to read these words. Many believe they were given by the great Shawnee Chief Tecumseh:

Live your life that the fear of death can never enter your heart. Trouble no one about their religion; respect others in their view, and demand that they respect yours. Love your life, perfect your life, beautify all things in your life. Seek to make your life long and its purpose in the service of your people. Prepare a noble death song for the day when you go over the great divide.

Always give a word or a sign of salute when meeting or passing a friend, even a stranger, when in a lonely place. Show respect to all people and grovel to none.

When you arise in the morning give thanks for the food and for the joy of living. If you see no reason for giving thanks, the fault lies only in yourself. Abuse no one and no thing, for abuse turns the wise ones to fools and robs the spirit of its vision.

When it comes your time to die, be not like those whose hearts are filled with the fear of death, so that when their time comes they weep and pray for a little more time to live their lives over again in a different way. Sing your death song and die like a hero going home.

I think this is a great example of an honor code. Tecumseh was a man in full possession of his King. What would your 'death song' be? When it's all said and done, what is most important to you? When it's your time to die, what will give you peace in your heart? How do you believe you should treat your fellow man? Your Core Values are different from your 'morals' or religious rules – those come from outside voices. Morals and religious rules are what you're 'supposed' to believe. Your Core Values are what you, in your heart of hearts, actually believe.

When you have clarity about your true purpose, your Core Values, and your honor code, your King knows how to move forward and knows how to weigh important decisions.

CORE VALUES

Take a moment to sit quietly with your notebook or journal. Make a list of at least eleven core values, ideas that you believe deeply in, that are worthy to be the guiding principles for your life's vision. Start the list with the words, 'I believe in.' After each of the core values, write an 'I statement' declaring what the principle means to you personally.

Below is a list of my Core Values to give you an idea of what I mean.

I believe in:

Service – I am always ready to serve with my time, body, mind, and spirit. I consider the position of servant to be the most honorable position.

Leadership – I take responsibility for my life, lead by example, and always try to bring out the best in others.

Family – I strive to be an excellent father and partner.

Brotherhood – I endeavor to always be available to support my universal brothers and sisters.

Honor – I live with a sense of respect for myself and others. I walk my talk and live my word.

Fearlessness – I refuse to be stopped by fear. I live in fearlessness and quell fear in others.

Love – Love is the lifeblood that connects us all. I live with my heart and am a servant and messenger of love. I am a heart healer.

Sensuality – I live through my senses. I enjoy and promote pleasure and beauty. I love the natural world and am fed by my connection to it.

Perseverance – I stay the course. I believe in grit and stick-to-it-ness. I believe that hardship in life is there to teach me and forge my metal. 'That which does not kill me makes me stronger.'

Vision – I am a man of vision, I consider my ability to create and manifest visions to be a supreme gift of the creator.

Spirit – I believe in a Great Spirit and am a man of prayer and meditation. I strive to experience the interconnectedness and sacredness of all things.

These are my Core Values. It would be hard for me to make a shorter list. I could easily make a longer one. I hope this gives you some idea of how to structure yours. What you put in yours might be very similar or totally different. The important thing is that it's completely true for you. And remember, 'Progress not perfection.' Don't get hung up if you don't live every one of your principles perfectly. Chances are that you don't. But your Core Values are essential items to know if you want to have a steady, powerful inner King.

3. BACKBONE

You've got a mission in life. You know what you stand for, and what you won't stand for. Because you have the inner Mystic too, you know your bullshit and what you'll fall for. When you have all this, you have what I call 'backbone.' As men, our backbone is what is profoundly true for us. It's what we believe in, it's a sense of what we will and won't budge on. Like the spine in the body, our backbone is the central axis of our integrity as a man. As we learn how to be potent and masculine again, we need to know how and where to direct our power. Big balls with no backbone is a bad combination.

When we have no backbone, or we have a weak one, and we lose our inner King, we usually become pleasers, servers. I'm not talking about being of service – serving is a powerful noble thing. I'm talking about being a slave, a puppet, being a drone or an object that is operated by others for their purposes, in the service of what is important to them – What does my woman want me to be? What does my mother want? What's going to keep me from getting fired? What's good enough? What will I settle for? What is easiest? What's going to make me feel comfortable in this moment?

BRUTAL HONESTY
What's Your Bullshit About the King?
What's your relationship to authority? How do
you feel in the presence of other powerful men?
Do you tend to doubt yourself? Do you identify as
an anti-authoritarian? Do you feel the need to
always criticize powerful or successful men? Or
can you admire them. Take a moment to examine all
of this for yourself. If you have issues with other
'Kings,' chances are you will have a hard time
embracing your own.

When we lack backbone these are the questions that define us. These questions become our guiding principles.

Your backbone is your self-knowledge. It's your self-respect and driving force in life.

Sometimes in our men's workshops and weekends we will talk about backbone as our 'True North.' When everything else has gone to shit, what is essential for us to salvage? All of this is crucial for man to know about himself.

I asked one of my young female clients what she found most attractive in a man. She considered it and replied emphatically, 'A man with a mission. A man who is totally focused on his mission in life. That passion turns me on. Also, if he's a little detached at the same time. Totally focused, but not obsessed or clinging.' She's describing the King. She's describing a man with backbone. Worth considering.

When you have this aspect of your King, people trust you, women want you, and enemies don't want to fuck with you.

Success in life comes to you, and you go to it. But if you're going to really strike out and claim your deep happiness and True Power, you'll need to flesh out a vision for your whole life.

4. VISION

Visioning

'Visioning' is one of the greatest skills you can develop. It isn't the same as planning. And it's not just 'dreaming' either. It's a practice of connecting to your inner King and choosing how you would like your life to be. Your vision then becomes more power for your inner King to make choices and set priorities in your life.

Visioning isn't just choosing anything that we want. For it to be powerful and really tap your King energy, your vision has be rooted in your true purpose and Core Values. You may think having a harem and owning a racing car would be nice, but chances are they don't really serve your true purpose, and might also violate your Core Values.

VISION

Take a moment with your journal or notebook and get quiet.

If you knew you couldn't fail, and keeping your true purpose and Core Values in mind, write out a short description of your vision for the following areas of your life:

WORK – This includes what you do for
a living, your professional success, your
professional relationships, your work-life
balance – anything important about your
work life.

PERSONAL RELATIONSHIPS – This includes
your friends, family, romantic relationships,
all of your personal connections with people.

MATERIAL ABUNDANCE – This is about your
money, your relationship to it, and the stuff
and lifestyle options that money affords.

INNER DEVELOPMENT – This is about who you
want to become on the inside, what you'd like
to learn, and how you want to approach your
life. This includes everything from inner
wounds you'd like to heal to your relationship
with Spirit, to mystical practice goals.

PHYSICAL HEALTH AND FITNESS – This is
about how you relate to your body, what you're
able to do with your body, and how you want to
feel in your body.

FUN AND ENJOYMENT – What would you most
like to do and enjoy in your free time? This is
an important part of visioning that men often
leave out.

Include at least three examples after each
section. The examples should be as specific
as possible, naming names and quantifying

amounts. For example: if you say in the relationships section that you envision having supportive, motivated friends, you should name people who are examples of what you're talking about. In your material abundance section, don't just say, 'I am wealthy' – state your annual salary or your net worth.

Enjoy the Process

Take time and have fun with this! If this is something new to you, let it be something new and don't get bogged down trying to do it perfectly. Let yourself suck at it at first. 'Embrace the suck' and keep going. Make each vision you write juicy. If it doesn't turn you on, it's not your vision and you're writing something you think you should want. Each section and each example should give you an inner smile and a feeling of 'Fuck, yeah!' Don't worry if it's not easy or perfect. And don't be afraid of commitment.

I come back to tweak my vision all the time. Your vision is a living thing that you're always tinkering with and adjusting. Just take an hour and hurl yourself into it and see what happens. If you give yourself to this exercise, even if you do it badly, you will get in touch with your inner King, and have a main component of the First Key to happiness and True Power.

When you've finished all the sections with examples, put it down in one document with your true purpose and Core Values. This document is your inner King's treasure.

BRUTAL HONESTY

In your journal, go back to the same six areas you visioned and write a gut-level honest assessment of the areas as they are currently. No blame, no shame - but you need to know where you're starting from. This is where you can look unflinchingly at your inner and outer bullshit and get your inner Warrior on the job to clean it up and start living into your vision.

5. THE FATHER

One of the aspects of the King is the Father. I don't mean dad. I mean the Father with a capital F — and I don't mean God either. When you get your King, you become a Father. It doesn't matter whether or not you have kids. When you have your King, you become a good Father to your life. There is a particular kind of love and protection that the Father represents. It's nourishing and protective at the same time. When you're the King, you're responsible for your realm. It's up to you to care for and protect the various things in your world. I'm not talking about the 'it's all up to me,' woe-is-me martyr act that disempowered dads do. I'm talking about a genuine sense of stewardship. You're responsible for your world, for your people's welfare. When you've got your King, and your King is rounded out by the other powers, you have a sense of power and completeness. Then your mantra becomes, 'I've got this.' Your partner, your children, your challenges, your inner child, your projects, your mission, your world ... has a King. Order's restored and everything flourishes.

SUMMING UP THE KING:

1. **True Purpose** – we have our King Power when we know our purpose and have that purpose in the center of our lives.

2. **Core Values** and **Honor Code** – to have the King, we need to know what we're about and what we deeply believe and hold sacred.

3. **Backbone** – there needs to be a part of every man that is unwavering and strong.

4. **Vision** – the King Power helps us hold on to our highest vision for life.

5. **The Father** – the King Power gives us the ability to be the loving, protecting, responsible father to our whole world.

Now that we have started to fire up your King energy, in the next chapter we are going to add the power and potency of your Warrior energy.

9

THE WARRIOR

O nce we have our King in place, once we have a good sense of our purpose in life, once we have our mission, we need some serious masculine power to make it all happen. We need balls to support our backbone. That's the role of our inner Warrior. The Warrior is the innate power every man has inside to get shit done, move forward, and stand up to challenges. The Warrior is the part of us that faces and defeats our inner enemies and outer obstacles. It's the inner Warrior's job to protect, serve, and make sure our mission happens. It is the Warrior that is charged with protecting the vision of the King and bringing that vision into reality, no matter how hard it is.

Most men today need more Warrior energy. Even typically 'tough' men or men with combat-oriented jobs need to tune up this aspect of their inner power. In general, men today have become passive. Many men are passive physically – modern life doesn't require us to do much with our bodies anymore. This same passivity shows up on an inner level too. We give up too many victories to our fears and weaknesses. We've lost the ability to stand our ground and fight the battles we need to fight; we let our life push us around.

WORRIERS, STRUGGLERS, AND WHINERS

Worriers

Instead of Warriors we have become worriers. When we don't face actual challenges in our outer life, we get consumed by the 'could be' and 'what if' challenges in our head. If there's something off in our life, we worry about it. We fret about it and hope it doesn't get worse. It's as if we can see a potential enemy approaching in the distance but respond by sitting there and hoping he doesn't arrive too soon. Warriors don't worry, they act. They ride out to meet the potential enemy and size him up. The Warrior tells the enemy to stop approaching, and if he doesn't halt, the Warrior stops him. Men without strong inner Warrior energy don't know how to set boundaries. They allow way too much bullshit into their life. Getting your inner Warrior is about getting out of your head and into your body. Out of the fantasy and into reality. Out of thinking about problems and into solving, attacking, and defeating problems.

Strugglers

Instead of Warriors we have become strugglers. Somewhere we have been led to believe that life is about constant struggle. You hear of men who struggle with a weight problem, depression, or their finances. You can struggle for a long time and there's no promise of relief. If we are strugglers, we were probably raised by strugglers that taught us that struggling is normal. Warriors don't struggle, they fight with everything they've got. They fight with excellence and masterful skill; they will win or lose. If a Warrior loses, he retreats, retrains, retools, and fights again with all he's got. He fights until he is triumphant. Too many men today have lost this sense of triumph. Finding your inner Warrior is about learning to fight for a triumphant life.

Whiners

Instead of Warriors we have become whiners. When our worrying and avoiding and struggling fail and we're actually faced with a challenge, we roll over and take it while we whine about it. When that enemy that we were worrying about gets to our village, we just go and get him some water, let him raid the village while we bitch and complain that it's not fair. The Warrior doesn't whine. He doesn't just talk about what he's gonna do or what he should do. He either does it, or he doesn't. In general the Warrior has less to complain about because he doesn't let the enemy get too close to begin with. He takes charge of his life and knows how to set and defend his boundaries.

Throttle Shy

There are many reasons why men abandon or ignore their inner Warrior energy. But the main reason is that we don't know how to use it. When I first started riding serious motorcycles such as Harley Davidsons, I was afraid of the throttle. I didn't really know how to ride big bikes, and the power in their huge engines scared the hell out of me. When I rode them I used the brakes too much and was very sheepish with the throttle. I was afraid that if I opened it up and unleashed the power of the engine, the bike would move too fast. I was worried that I would lose control and crash. I thought avoiding the throttle would keep me from harm. As I got more training and practice and became more comfortable handling the machine, I learned to love the throttle. I love being able to make the motorcycle move quickly if it needs to. And I've also learned that the throttle is as important for safety as the brakes. You need to be able to throttle up and evade hazards, and going much slower than traffic on a motorcycle is downright dangerous. I think a lot of us feel the same about our masculine powers. Deep down, we know that our strong male energies can be dangerous. And they can be, if we don't know how to operate them. But it's also dangerous when we fail to operate them. We don't crash from going too fast; we crash because we can't get out of the way of traffic. If we disown our Warrior, we are in danger of not living our Truth.

Rambo

Lots of 'intelligent' men shy away from Warrior energy if it seems to be too macho. They associate Warrior energy with shallow cartoon machismo. They think of Rambo or other tough guys in movies. As we start owning our power it's important that we remember that we're connecting *our* Warrior energy, not someone else's. There are all kinds of ideas of what Warrior energy should look like. Tough guys, hard guys, stoic guys, intense guys; for us to really travel our Red Road, it's up to us to find our unique expression of Warrior energy and bring it out in a way that is authentic to us. It's not about imitating some idea of toughness, it's about digging in and finding the action-oriented, passionate, unstoppable aspect of our own self.

The Warrior energy is not something we need to get from outside. It's an innate energy that flows in our blood. All of us. Inside of every one of us is a hunter, a soldier, a weapon-wielding, fearless, protecting, killing Warrior. It's an archetype, an innate power that we're born with. To get the Three Keys intact, you need this power up and running. The Warrior is the part of you that will keep you on track with your vision. It is also the part that will give you the discipline needed to really make progress in a spiritual practice. And for getting free from bullshit, you need to be fearless to face it all and fierce to break through and really get free.

> *Question:* How tough, how strong, how fierce does your Warrior energy have to be?
> *Answer:* How big is your vision? How tough are the inner and outer obstacles that are in your way?

If your Warrior Power is intact and in balance, you will hold the key to owning your Violence and Grit, and you will learn to face Danger, Fear, Pain, and Challenge.

1. VIOLENCE

Every boy, guy, and man carries in them a parcel of violence. No matter who we are or what kind of man we've become, we have within us the blood of a Warrior, the blood of a hunter, the blood of a fearsome protector. Whether or not we ever actually engage in real violence, we all have this energy within us. It's part of our hard-wiring. This inner violence is something that few intelligent men are really comfortable with. As we own our inner Warrior, we need to come to grips with our violent energy. It's not bad; it's totally natural and necessary. Without the capacity for violence, our ancestors would not have been able to feed their families or defend their property, let alone create nations and advanced civilizations. In our modern life, we can learn to harness this energy to create our ideal life and drive away distractions and obstacles.

Some men are more in touch with this aspect of themselves than others. Some men get into martial arts, firearms, hunting, or military careers. These men can live out some of their Warrior energies through these outer behaviors. But even the cops and soldiers and tough-guy bikers I work with struggle with this violent aspect of their masculinity.

Most men today have very little outlet for their violent energies — or even awareness of them. We might enjoy watching violence on a screen, or the vicarious battles of spectator sports; we might like the bombing and shooting and fighting in video games, but still be out of touch with our own deep violence.

This energy is physical. This violence is not mental — it lives as a potential for violence in our body, in our muscles and nervous system. When someone threatens or insults us or pisses us off, a reaction stirs in us. There is something in us that wants to strike, strangle, or even kill the offender. Of course, a man of honor will learn to channel his violence so as not to harm people around him. A Warrior knows how to wield force skillfully. But misdirecting our violence isn't the problem. The problem is when we disown or squash these energies. When this happens we become downright passive. Many men today suffer from this condition. They lack even the most basic sense of action, let alone a war-making, spear-chucking, mammoth-hunting Warrior spirit.

> When someone threatens or insults us or pisses us off, a reaction stirs in us. There is something in us that wants to strike, strangle, or even kill the offender.

The Warrior

I'm not saying that we need to go out and buy weapons or start hunting or brawling. Not at all. I'm saying that we need to acknowledge this aspect of ourselves and honor it, and learn to direct its intense energy towards our purpose and vision. This intensity, this inner violence we all have in our genes, in our cells, gives our inner Warrior potency.

When we don't own or operate this aspect of the Warrior skillfully, we either become the passive struggler, worrier, or whiner, or our natural male aggressive energy comes out sideways in unhealthy and unhelpful ways. We get grumpy, or we rage at the people closest to us. In the most extreme cases it comes out in actual misplaced physical violence. We beat our families, or get into bar fights. We road rage. A cop who doesn't own his inner Warrior will use too much force when arresting someone. A middle manager or office guy might act out his disowned violence by being petty, writing people up on stupid violations, or being generally nasty with his underlings and co-workers. A bureaucrat out of touch with his Warrior will become the proverbial 'ball buster' – the guy who always says no, or who makes things unnecessarily hard for people. If we don't know how to channel our inner violence, we become naysayers, or we're mean to animals, or we live in a generally angry way. We become toxic. We create an ugly world where delicate things cannot survive. A Warrior owns his inner violence and uses it to protect the delicate things in his world. He uses his intensity to serve his mission and fight for his vision.

Some men who have disowned violence are 'hot heads'; they are known for their temper and people steer clear of them when they're angry. Everyone tiptoes around the volatile, moody guy and avoids speaking the truth. These men will either push everyone away or attract only passive people who avoid any confrontation.

When we own this inner aspect of ourselves as men and really learn to use it well, we are cooler than the average man. We are less likely to lose our temper and more likely to command situations in our life. Others know not to fuck with us, but they also are not afraid that we're going to freak out or lash out.

These are all examples of the violent energy coming out in unhealthy ways; sometimes it doesn't come out at all.

If a man really denies this side of himself he becomes passive, like a neutered animal. He's soft, he has no teeth, no ability to say no, or stick up for himself. This is what Robert Bly called the 'soft male.' This sort of guy is susceptible to all kinds of shit – oppression, depression, and exploitation. The modern corporate/political world depends on men not having any teeth. I don't know how the corporate world would work if all men found their inner Warrior.

My dad was like that. He couldn't stand up to my mother. She was the only one that was allowed to have the violent energy in our family. She wielded it in her toxic, critical bitchiness. She would nag and whine at him, and Dad would just slump in his lazy boy, drink martinis, watch TV, and let time slip by.

People who are into holistic medicine think that repressed, unexpressed, violent energy might be the cause of illnesses like cancer. If the killer in us isn't expressed outwardly, it expresses itself inward and kills us.

Depression and illness aside, the main casualty of the disowned Warrior is our life and mission. We need that healthy hunter-killer-warrior energy to fight for what's important to us and to stand up against the bullshit in life that wants to distract us from our purpose. If we want deep happiness and True Power, we need the ability to fight, not in a bar, but at the office, or with our inner enemies in our

> The Inner Warrior gives us passion, and passion is essential for men to live with backbone.

meditation room. A man needs to be able to fight for his family, for his relationship. A man needs to be able to say no. He needs to be able to stand up to his woman without freaking out or being a dick. Having backbone means being able to make hard decisions, and being fearless in the face of conflict and threat. We need the ability to 'kick ass and take names' in our work, in our community, in our spiritual life – to accomplish our mission and live in our vision. The Inner Warrior gives us passion, and passion is essential for men to live with backbone.

2. GRIT

Grit is the quality the Warrior gives us to stay the course, to give us backbone when things are tough. I don't like to think about being 'tough.' I think of tough meat or a calloused heart. In the Lover chapter we'll learn about being soft when it's time to be soft. But here we need to talk about getting hard. Part of being a man is facing the hard stuff of life. Our grit is our ability to stand up against whatever is thrown at us without giving up or giving in. Grit is our ability to 'embrace the suck' in a hard situation and keep going. It's our ability to be knocked down and get back up without losing track of where we're going.

> *Everyone has a plan until they get punched in the face.*
> Mike Tyson

If we're really living our vision, we will get punched in the face again and again. Unless we're playing very small we have to learn to realize our vision through a process of trial and error. And this can be like being in the ring with a big sweaty prizefighter. If you have your King and you're pretty clear about your mission and Core

Values, you've got a great start. But once you get into the nitty-gritty of actually doing the things in your vision, you're gonna get hit. If you're trying to live a big life, you're going to get knocked down and get the wind knocked out of you. And that's when you need grit.

As a species, we humans have become soft in the last 200 years. We don't need to do much hard stuff anymore. We don't hunt, we don't farm, we don't slaughter, we don't build, we don't fight. At least you could say that most of us don't have to do any of these things. We turn on the tap – clean water flows. Turn on your furnace – you've got heat. Want to eat the meat of a 700lb animal? Pick up your phone and have

> If you're trying to live a big life, you're going to get knocked down and get the wind knocked out of you. And that's when you need grit.

it delivered, cooked and ready to go with fries and a Coke. Most men today couldn't even cut up a potato and deep-fry it, let alone plant, grow, and harvest one.

A man walking the Red Road needs grit. And, in general, most modern men lack this essential quality. I think it's a generational thing. Even the most domesticated men of past generations knew how to change the oil in their car or build a fire in the woods. They knew the value of hard work and didn't cry too much if they had to do something that really sucked. They didn't expect life to be easy, and would step forward to accept difficult challenges when others could not. Part of what helped the men of previous generations – I think – was mandatory military service. My dad, born in 1925, was a suit-wearing, mild-mannered, passive guy in most regards, but if he had to, he knew how to bayonet a man. Once upon a time he had a drill sergeant yelling in his face and had to belly-crawl through mud with a rifle. He may have walked a Black Road and 'lived small,' but he was no pussy. Dad had grit.

Dad was born into a generation that sacrificed through world wars and revolutions, and got their grit as a matter of course. He was of a generation of men who assumed they would offer their coat to a lady, or carry a heavy load for her, or stand up to a bully if need be. I, born in 1971, have had to learn to get grit. I've had to learn how to do hard stuff, sometimes going out of my way to do so.

How's your grit? What happens to you when you get punched in the face?

3. DANGER

The Warrior in us gives us the ability to be steady in the face of danger. Our sense of danger is not the same as our sense of fear. Fear is a mental thing. Fear is an emotional reaction to thoughts about potential risk or danger. Our sense of danger is a valuable situational awareness we have in the present moment. The Warrior knows how to act in the presence of danger.

There's a beautiful thing that happens when we allow ourselves to embrace risk and danger. There's a rush, a flood of supportive energy that sharpens our senses and puts fire in our body. When our Warrior is disowned or weak, we avoid anything dangerous or risky and miss out on this life-giving energy. And when real danger does arise, we freeze or flop. Traditionally, men have even sought out dangerous kinds of play to hone this aspect of

> When we connect to that fearless, danger-facing energy, we are owning our inner Warrior.

themselves. Male animals will play-fight with each other. They are not just learning to hunt, they are expressing something innate. It's good to know how to handle yourself in the face of danger, and it's good to be a little dangerous.

Most men today avoid anything acutely dangerous – or at least that's what they think. They eat bad food and risk heart attack, drive cars, smoke, drink alcohol, and sit idly by while their spouse loses interest in them. They are fine with all these kinds of danger – that's not what I mean. I am talking about taking conscious risks for the sake of something good. It could be simply risk for fun or adventure, or it could be risk for the sake of growth and success. When we connect to that fearless, danger-facing energy, we are owning our inner Warrior.

Midlife Danger

Men going through a 'midlife crisis' will seek out danger. They might start riding motorcycles, or having illicit sex with women that endangers their marriage, or start taking other risks. From my point of view, most if not all of the behaviors that society writes off as 'midlife crisis' are repressed, healthy male impulses coming to the surface. I see the midlife crisis as less like a crisis and more like a man coming to his senses. Of course he wants to have great sex. Of course he wants to drive a great car, buy a gun, and start wearing leather jackets. If he didn't let himself do all of that when he was younger, if he suppressed it and settled down, and did what others wanted him to do, then it's natural for it to erupt. In his forties something kicks in – a sense of time's urgency, maybe. Or maybe he has some success by then and gets a glimpse of his bigness and wants more. Sometimes it's just money. Many of us can't afford to buy the motorcycle until we're in our midlife. Anyway, I'm simply saying that these eruptions aren't all bad. Many men are really clumsy at this stage in their life. Many do make fools of themselves and fuck lots of things up. But at least they're coming alive. Other men aren't lucky enough to even have these energies stir at midlife.

When this kind of thing happens consciously, it's a downright wonderful thing. I coach a lot of men through beautiful moments of midlife awakening. The secret to making it a healthy movement is all of this other backbone work that we're doing. Without the other self-development, what typically happens is that a man will have that awakening/crisis, go crazy, blow off all that repressed steam, and then go back to being just a half-awake guy again.

Make it Count

Many men get a lot out of doing something a little dangerous in their playtime – like surfing or mountain climbing or motorcycling. It's not about being reckless or 'playing with fire.' It's not about seeking out danger. It's about being able to face and mitigate (overcome) the danger. When I ride my motorcycle, I know that the way I ride and the awareness I bring to the ride is a matter of life and death. Believe me, I am super cautious and train my ass off so that I am minimizing the chances of going 'rubber side up.' The thrill of riding comes because I am doing something potentially dangerous – lethal, actually – but using my skill, wisdom, and situational awareness to make it safe and enjoyable. When I started riding, it was terrifying. I used to joke about wearing a diaper under my leather riding gear for the moments when I shit my pants. Now I can think of few things that give more enjoyment than blazing down the highway. But there is a lethal intensity: what I do and don't do counts.

These days most of us avoid do-or-die situations. Most men don't even go near physical danger; more importantly, the same goes for taking risks in love, business, or in their life journey. When we always play it safe, we may stay out of harm's way, but our inner Warrior is suffocated. If we never leave our comfort zones and take the risks we need to take, we don't grow or learn. Our life can make us weaker instead of stronger. Our King becomes a mere dreamer. He's got no army. The great lion's got no teeth.

When we have our inner Warrior intact, our King's vision has a 'fighting chance' of being realized. We have the grit and guts we need to stay on our path and stay in the fight. To embrace this inner Warrior energy we need to change our relationship to fear, pain, and challenge.

4. FEAR

Fear is something that holds most people down. When we embrace our inner Warrior energy, we learn how to eliminate the bogus mental fears that plague most people, and we learn to embrace and overcome the 'danger response' that happens as we take risks and go for the big life.

Any new situation will cause the 'danger response' — it's supposed to. When something new happens, our body goes on alert. Imagine walking through the forest and coming upon a bear. Our heart rate increases, our breath changes, our eyes get super focused. We're ready to run, or fight, or freeze. It's hard-wired into us and every other mammal. That whole response is there to help us survive our meeting with the bear. Our problem in modern life is that we have this response but there's no

> A man with real backbone doesn't avoid something just because he's afraid of it.

bear! We have this response to a meeting with a boss, to a new relationship, or to a new venture. We have this response when we try something new or risky in the pursuit of our vision. But instead of the response giving us the power boost we need to overcome whatever is presented to us, it cripples us. It becomes a punch in the face.

The Warrior knows how to turn that paralyzing fear into useable energy. Instead of being afraid, we're 'stoked.' Instead of saying 'Oh no!' we say 'Here we go!' Instead of feeling stuck and holding back, we get stoked, find our grit, and enter the fray. A man with real backbone doesn't avoid something just because he's afraid of it.

5. PAIN

Most of the time when we're afraid, we're afraid of some kind of pain. As a race, we are terrified of pain and have an overall inability to handle it: mental, physical, or otherwise. There are massive pain-avoidance industries in the Western world. Think about it: the alcohol industry, the pharmaceutical industry, the entertainment industry. In our modern life, one thing we never need to go without is some way to numb or avoid our pain. The Warrior is not a masochist – someone who gets off on pain. But he's not stopped by his pain either.

The Warrior in us teaches us that pain is often just part of doing important things. But the Warrior also knows how to distinguish between that kind of pain and the pain that's telling us something is not right and needs to be changed. If you've ever tried to transform your body, you know that if you're not willing to face some pain, you'll never progress in making your body stronger. The same thing goes for life. Elite military units like the

US Navy Seals say that 'pain is weakness leaving the body.' In their case they're talking about their rigorous physical training, but the same thing goes for the heart/mind/life training that we do on our path to deep happiness and backbone. If we're not willing to face some pain, we will never realize our vision.

The more we sweat in peace, the less we bleed in war.
General George S Patton

6. CHALLENGE

Challenge is the other thing we need to make friends with. If something is difficult, that's not a reason to not do it. In fact, to the Warrior, challenge is a good thing. If we continually do the easy thing, we will only become weaker. When we avoid a challenge, or lose our grit and back off when something gets hard, we not only miss out on the resistance training that getting through the hard stuff gives us, we also lose a bit of self-respect. Think about a challenging situation and how you would feel if you didn't face it to see what I mean: Do something challenging, anything – and don't give up until you get through, overcome, and triumph. You will be stronger for staying with it; the next challenge will seem easier. And you'll enjoy that feeling that is all too scarce these days: pride.

Pride has gotten a bad reputation in the modern psychoanalytic age. Pride is usually thought of as a kind of egoist stupidity or shallow arrogance. But there's a difference between foolish pride and true pride. True pride is a core quality of a Warrior. We earn pride by sticking to our guns when things get hard. We

True pride is a core quality of a Warrior.

earn pride by living by our core principles, even when we're knocked down and bleeding. It's the pride of a person who finished the triathlon, or the dissertation, or didn't give up on their kid. It's the pride of a craftsman who still cares and does his work the hard way.

BRUTAL HONESTY

Make a list of your fears. Include at least ten. Figure out how you can change your feeling from fear to exhilaration: From 'Oh no' to 'Here we go!' If you want to 'get into' the fears and look at where they're from, go ahead. But the main thing is to figure out how you can get stoked to face the fears.

Make a list of pains you have to face as you go about living your vision. List at least ten and figure out what you need to do to 'embrace the suck' and embrace the pain as a necessary toll on the Red Road to deep happiness and True Power.

Make a list of the top challenges that are a part of your vision. Again, think of at least ten and visualize and describe how it will feel to stay the course and triumph in them. What strengths will you build, what kind of pride will you feel?

STEPPING OFF THE CURB

One day, as I was coming out of meditation, I had a vision and an insight that rocked my world. As my memory began to stir, I saw in my mind's eye the face of a kid I'd known in high school,

Tony. I hadn't thought of Tony in decades! And here he was in my meditation room. I have learned to pay attention to these post-meditation visions, so I contemplated Tony and got a potent and ass-kicking life lesson.

Tony was a black kid in the same grade as me, and he was a little unusual. Most of the black kids in our school were into hip-hop music, sports, and typical urban culture. There were street gangs in our town and many of the black kids identified with the gangs. Tony was different. He was from a working-class family like many of the other kids, but he wasn't into that culture. Tony was into heavy metal and smoking dope and playing bass in a cover band. Instead of wearing the standard urban uniform of the day, Tony wore band shirts and spiked wristbands with skinny jeans and tall boots. He was taller than most of the kids in our class, but he wasn't into basketball or any sports. Tony caught a lot of shit from the other kids – especially the other young black males. I was a stoner, so I had a natural alliance with the metalheads. I knew Tony because I smoked cigarettes in the bathroom with him.

When I contemplated my vision, I remembered coming out after school one day to see a crowd of kids gathered around the parking lot of the school. Our high school had a big parking lot ringed by a circular curb. All the kids were lined up around the circle, watching and cheering. I ran up to see what everyone was looking at. As I got to the curb I saw that in the middle of the big circle were two young gangbangers picking a fight with Tony. They were pushing him back and forth trying to pick a fight. Everyone was cheering for one side or the other. It was horrible; Tony was scared: he was clearly going to get his ass kicked.

I stood there on the curb, watching and really wanting to help him. He wasn't a good friend or anything but he didn't deserve this. The bullying progressed to the point where they started punching him in the head and face. I wanted to do something, but I stayed right where I was on the curb with the other kids. Soon they had Tony on the ground, beating his head on the cement parking block. I stayed where I was and watched. Everyone did. Eventually the gangbangers left him alone, or a teacher came out – I don't remember which. They didn't kill him but they beat the shit out of him and surely humiliated him badly. I don't remember what I did after. I guess I went home or went and got stoned or something.

As I sat in my meditation room and remembered this story I realized that I don't know what would have happened if I had stepped off that curb to help Tony that day. And I never will know.

I could have stepped off the curb and inspired 20 other kids to do the same and stop the bullying. I could have stepped off the curb and gotten my own ass kicked along with Tony. Stepping off might not have changed much of the outcome but it could have made a big difference to Tony's heart. Stepping off may have made a difference to the bullies. But ... I will never know. What I do know is that whatever would have happened, including having my own ass kicked, would have been worth it. Whatever had happened then, today I would be glad I did it. But I will never know. The thought that I stood there and watched a friend get beat up like that makes me sick. It makes me feel shame and remorse and regret. There will be no re-take for that exam.

If your sword's too short, add to its length by taking one step forward.

Anonymous

There are so many moments like this in life. So what can we learn from them? Surely it's not just about feeling bad. It's easy to feel regret without really learning much. I think it's about learning to recognize the ways in which we are standing on the curb today. Often when we're faced with a challenge, especially one that involves danger or risk, we choke and get paralyzed by fear of the short-term consequences and lose sight of the bigger picture. We lose sight of what and who we are. In this case, I was afraid of a whole host of short-term consequences: getting beat up, being embarrassed, becoming an enemy of the gang, etc. It's not as if I thought it through in the moment – we rarely do. It's just a sort of base fear, avoidance, and paralysis. Many of us learn this behavior when we're young. Our dads and other adult males probably model this kind of thing to us. As the years on the curb go by, a sticky, flabby habit of non-action keeps us on the curb and out of the fray. But the fray just may be where we want to be.

Getting in touch with our inner Warrior energies is about getting in touch with that part of us that is ready to step off the curb, move forward, and take a stand when it's time to take a stand.

Spiritual people will say that on a cosmic level, on the level of 'God's will' and destiny, everything just flows the way it is 'meant to.' I believe this, I really do. But on the ground it seems that what makes the difference when it comes to being awake and fully alive is what we choose to do in this sort of moment. Are we willing to risk failing, or do we choose to be safe and not take the chance? Also I do realize that I used an example of something that involved violence. That situation was actually dangerous. It wasn't like I was just afraid to speak up or share my heart's true feelings. There was a serious risk of be getting my ass kicked, as badly – if not worse – than Tony. I am not advocating dangerous risk-taking behavior. But allow your Warrior to stand up once in a while – even if it seems a little dangerous.

> Getting in touch with our inner Warrior energies is about getting in touch with that part of us that is ready to step off the curb.

The only way we'll ever know is if we wade into the fray and see for ourselves.

The edge is a funny thing, the only people who know where it is are the ones who have gone over it.

Hunter S Thompson

EMBRACING THE SUCK

How can you shift from fear to exhilaration? Make a list of the challenges you're facing in your life right now. What if they were all there to give you some resistance training? What strength is the universe trying to instill in you?

WHAT ABOUT YOU?

The first step in all of this is the owning step. Take some time to simply reflect on this aspect of your manhood. How do you relate to violence and the idea of 'the Warrior'? In what ways does violence show up in your life? Are you violent in your actions or words? Do you tend to simmer with anger or explode? Are you comfortable saying no when you need to? Do you stand up for yourself in your relationship, in your workplace, in your community? Have you really disowned and squashed you inner Warrior? Have a look. No blame, no shame, just have a look.

Do you tend to go toward your problems, attack and fight, or do you tend to withdraw and just think about what you woulda/shoulda/coulda done?

What was modeled to you as a boy? How were the older men in terms of their inner violence? How was your dad? When you were little were you a tough kid or a wimp? Did you get beatings or give them or avoid fights altogether? There are no right answers here. It's just about getting to know yourself and how much Warrior energy you have tucked away down there.

As I see it, it's good news or good news: if you have your inner Warrior intact, that's great because it means you have this important element of your inner power ready to go. If you don't, that's still good news because it means that things are only going to get better. The awakening of the inner Warrior is a great thing to witness in a man. The Warrior brings with him great power and intensity and testosterone.

Recent studies at Columbia and Harvard tested men's testosterone levels and then had them simply take on more upright, slightly aggressive postures, and then tested them again. Every time, there was a boost in the men's 'T' levels. It isn't about stupid chest thumping and acting tough, but it is about allowing yourself to embrace and express tougher, more primal, more 'dangerous' ways of being.

BRUTAL HONESTY

What's Your Bullshit About the Warrior?

Look at the ways that you might have some baggage around this aspect of yourself. Do you feel like a wimp? Were you bullied? Do you oppose war or find violent things distasteful in some way? Do you identify as someone who isn't into it? Or are you stuck in the other side? Do you over-identify with the Warrior? Are you stuck being a tough guy and have an inability to be soft or appreciate beauty?

LETTING THE BEAST OFF THE LEASH

When you've gotten a sense of where you stand with these energies, then I suggest you start to cultivate ways to exercise them. That means giving them an outlet, but also making them stronger. You might find some kind of competitive contact sport that you enjoy, or take up some kind of 'danger hobby' like hiking in the mountains, or motorcycling, or horseback riding. One of the men I work with works behind a desk in a big tech company during the week. On the weekend he takes care of his inner Warrior by surfing in the ocean. He tells me that part of the appeal of surfing is the danger involved. There's an awe and fear that comes from being in something as massive as the ocean. He exerts his body and his skill completely.

> The awakening of the inner Warrior is a great thing to witness in a man.

Many men find some kind of martial arts training is a good way to feed their inner Warrior. This could be Kung Fu or Capoeira, but it could also mean learning archery or shooting. Most gyms have punching bags; learn how to punch one, or take a kick-boxing class. Get your blood pumping and see how it feels to hit, kick, or shoot something.

Rage

Rage is not an emotion, it is a physical energy, and an important one for men to have a handle on. I make sure that every man I work with has at least one place and regular moment in his life where he can really let go and express rage. Many men find they have a kind of pent-up rage in their body that they need to release. It isn't anger about something exactly; it's the collective physical energy stirred up by various life pressures. When something pisses us off, thwarts us, or threatens our mission, there is a deep part of us that wants to react violently. When we are in our houses with our families, there is a part of us that knows that we are the most dangerous thing in the house. We keep ourselves on a kind of leash. It's the same thing within the professional world, or modern society in general. Any honest father will tell you there have been times when he wanted to smack his kids, or punch his wife. Many among us have fantasized about murdering people at work. I hope you don't smack the kids, or beat the wife, or stab the boss. But that fiery energy has to go somewhere. It turns into rage and we need to release it.

Video games, even the most violent ones, only express the mental rage. Team sports help us release a little bit, but we have to play within the rules and be part of a team. What I'm describing is really best done in private. It's not rational, it's totally primal, animal. It can only come out with primal, physical, explosive action.

Increase the intensity of your workout. If you don't already have a workout, get one. Make times in your week when you can go all-out and sweat and grunt and feel your strength. Howl, break stuff, chop wood, throw heavy things, blast off as many push-ups as you can. I cannot over emphasize the importance of venting your rage. For men on the Red Road, push-ups are as important as meditation – maybe even more important. Next time you're up against something hard and feeling frustrated or anxious or fearful, drop down and pound out 10–30 push-ups as fast as you can. You'll be amazed at the effect.

If you have a place where you can scream or howl without having the cops called, you might want to try that too.

When you've owned your inner Warrior, that chunk of violent energy we all have somewhere down in our belly, then it is less likely to haunt you, hound you, or make you mean, sick, or abusive.

Outbursts like road rage or freak-out moments vented on our kids or loved ones are expressions of impotence, not potency. If we own our own intense, primal, spear-chucking, hunter-killer energy, then we can have access to that intensity and harness it and direct it in a way that serves our ultimate purpose. We possess a kind of cool badass quality that is not just posturing. We have a thump. We can feel it and take comfort in it. Others can feel it too. People trust us more; they don't want to fuck with us. Kids, women, and vulnerable people feel protected by us. It's a great thing.

Then it's time to take a look at the various quadrants of your life and see where that badass quality is needed. Where do you need to be more fearsome, more fearless? Where do you need to show your sword and even swing it?

Don't be a Pussy

People give me a lot of shit for saying the P-word. Women especially hate it when I use it. Boys were teased and called pussies on the playground. I used to feel the same way, but I have grown to really like it. We have reclaimed the word in our men's group and use it to challenge each other. In this context, a pussy is someone who has not only disowned their inner Warrior, but who is – in some way – being a coward. Even 'coward' is a charged word. But we need these words because there are those aspects in all of us that are really not working for us. When we say 'stop being a pussy' to each other in our group, it means, 'Remember your strength and live from that strength.' It's a way to call each other out when we are cowering and not moving forward with our vision because of fear or because we don't want to leave our comfort zone. Not being a pussy means being the King. It means remembering our power and our intention for life. It means to remember what we're about and stop acting like we don't know.

It's so important to learn to support each other as men in a masculine way. We can cry with each other, and let go and open up about our weakness and life messes, but if we do it with our men, we have to then also hear them say, 'And don't be a pussy about it. Man up and take care of your mess!' Men offer a different kind of shoulder to cry on. It might take some getting used to at first.

In general I think it's important to take back these playground insults. I think it's good to remind ourselves to 'man up' or 'stop being a pussy' or 'grow a pair.' Because when we do it in this context, in the context of owning our wild, mature, masculine fullness, we are not doing it in a stupid, brutish, macho way. It's good to not be so thin-skinned and easily offended. Men with backbone need to be able to knock each other around a little bit and not get upset about it.

DON'T DO IT ALONE

To own our inner Warrior, we don't just need to change our relationship to fear, challenge, and pain; we also need to change our relationship to teamwork. A Warrior will only train or engage an enemy alone if he absolutely has to. Even elite military snipers work in teams. The Warrior is not a hero. The hero is an immature version of the Warrior – he runs in, saves the day all alone and shines with glory. It doesn't matter to a Warrior how it looks. It doesn't matter what glory or recognition he gets. Most Warriors get little or none. The Warrior is about getting the job done. The Warrior is about purpose, and the best way to achieve a purpose is to marshal the maximum amount of power available.

Every man needs a team. Warriors know how to work together with other Warriors and also do their job within a chain of command. This is a hard pill for many modern men to swallow.

There are always men who have more power, more know-how, or more perspective than we do. If we are to be effective Warriors, we need to know how to use the resources offered by others and even take orders sometimes.

The Warrior is not a brute. The Warrior is a master. His energy is not a threat, it is essential. That's the whole point here. We are reclaiming our masculine energies in a conscious, intelligent, masterful way and wielding them in the name of our high vision of service, excellence, and robust living.

If we are to live our vision and get through the bullshit and obstacles of life, we must be Warriors, we must own this part of ourselves. And when we do, our whole life benefits.

SUMMING UP THE WARRIOR

The Warrior – the innate power every man has inside to get shit done, move forward, and stand up to challenges.

What's Stopping your Warrior – when we're out of touch with our Warrior we become worriers, strugglers, and whiners.

Sometimes we avoid our inner Warrior because we're afraid of its power, or we're afraid of becoming a macho jerk.

The Warrior Power:

1. Owns **Violence** – men in touch with their Warrior own their violence and know how to channel their rage.
2. Has **Grit**
3. Faces **Danger**
4. Uses **Fear**
5. Faces **Pain**
6. Takes up **Challenges** with Pride

Allow your Warrior to Come Forward – step off the curb and look at your bullshit about the Warrior.

Let the Beast off the Leash – vent rage and don't be a pussy.

Don't Do it Alone – Warriors work in teams whenever they can.

BRUTAL HONESTY

In your journal or on your computer, take a moment to get quiet and reflect on your life as a man. Close your eyes and imagine yourself going through a typical day. Watch yourself as if you're watching a character in a movie.

When you're not using your Warrior, how do you act? If you're not in your bigness, what kind of smallness do you tend to gravitate toward?

Try to have compassion and a sense of humor about what you see. Capture it in your journal or notebook.

Now that you have started to connect to your Warrior energy, in the next chapter we are going to visit the Mystic – the power of your Spirit, consciousness, and innate wisdom.

10

THE MYSTIC

The Mystic is the power of our consciousness. It is both the power of our intellect and wisdom, and also our spiritual intelligence and ability to cultivate a rich spiritual life.

The core value of the Mystic is to be the seer and keeper of your vision. Wise kings always have spiritual advisors. Our King Power needs a strong inner Mystic to keep our vision pure and strong. Traditional kings would rely heavily on the advice of gurus, astrologers, and clerics. Think of King Arthur and his wizard advisor Merlin. The Mystic is also the wisdom and 'cool head' that balances the Warrior's 'let's do it' mentality. If the King represents the top command, and the Warrior represents the operations unit, the Mystic is the intelligence wing. Remember, we're after a balanced expression of our masculine power, and for the Second Key to

> The core value of the Mystic is to be the seer and keeper of your vision.

Happiness we need a deep and authentic spiritual connection. To have that, we need to have our inner game in good shape.

If your Mystic Power is intact and in balance, you will hold the key to its three aspects: the Wise Man, the Shaman, and the Medicine Man. You'll also gain the Superpowers that enable you to see below the surface of things, to have clarity of mind and recognize beauty, and to stay clear of bullshit.

1. THE WISE MAN

Traditionally a whole man was expected to be wise – along with being strong and fearless. When I speak of wisdom here, I'm not talking about book knowledge or intellectual knowledge. I'm not talking about knowing facts or being good at trivia games or sports statistics. I'm talking about life-knowledge. You can gain ordinary knowledge by studying. You can go on the internet and collect facts and ideas. To gain wisdom, you have to live. You can study wisdom – read the *Bhagavad Gita* or Plato. You can listen to others' wisdom – sit at the feet of great teachers or elders. But in order to make any wisdom your own, to have it written in your bones, you have to live your life and try to apply that wisdom.

In the traditional Indian system of learning, there are three stages: *shravana*, *manana*, and *nidhidhyasana*. Shravana means to hear: we have to really hear a teaching, or really be present at a life event and 'get' what it is trying to teach us. Then comes manana: we have to memorize the teaching, we have to work with it, practice it, use it, test it in our lives. Finally, when that process is complete, we arrive at nidhidhyasana. This is when the teaching has become a part of us. We don't even need to think about it because it has become a part of our very fiber as men. This is true for ordinary learning – like learning to drive a car – and it's equally true for learning life lessons – like learning to keep your mouth shut when it's time to be quiet, or learning to speak your truth when it's time to make a noise.

A whole man, a happy man with backbone, is in possession of his wisdom. Like the money we have in the bank, we should also have a store of wisdom. Many men disown this part of themselves.

> Wisdom is power. If we are to be powerful and happy, we need to be as wise as we can possibly be.

Sometimes men feel it's not cool to be the smart kid in class. Immature guys don't care about wisdom or learning. They might apply themselves to school or any professional training they are subjected to, but they aren't so concerned about cultivating deep wisdom. They are more focused on entertainment and recreation. Men who are stuck in their hard-guy mode might discount the Wise Man energy: They don't want to use their hearts or their minds – they want action! Wisdom is power. If we are to be powerful and happy, we need to be as wise as we can possibly be.

Don't Get Stuck in your Head

Of course, there are many men around today who are overly stuck in their heads. Modern intelligent men lean way too much on their intellect. Maybe when they were younger they were the smart kids who were bullied by the jocks. Now their intellect or education has put them in a dominant place. When I was a kid I always felt I was smarter than my enemies, smarter than my teachers and parents, and I took refuge in that. But being smart and being wise are two different things.

Nowadays there is a whole other way that men get stuck in their head: the internet. So many of us spend so much time online relating to a pixelated world and relatively little time living with our actual bodies in the material world. The internet itself won't make us stupid, but it can definitely contribute in that it keeps us disconnected from our bodies and in our heads.

Living Wisdom

When we talk about the role of the Wise Man part of our Mystic Power on the path toward having real backbone, we're talking about honoring our intelligence and wisdom, and having a connection to that wise, mature, masculine part of our psyche for the sake of living a robust, full-throttle life. It's not about being more brainy or in our heads. It's about learning to honor and harness and utilize our intelligence for the sake of our purpose. When I was a young teacher, I thought I knew everything. I was full of beans and on fire to help people, but I was young and lacked seasoning. One day one of my mentors – a senior monk – called me into his chambers and sat me down and told me the following story:

> Once a young ram and an old ram were standing on a hill looking down at a meadow full of sheep. The young ram said to the old ram, 'Hey! I've got an idea! Let's run down the hill and fuck one of those sheep!'
>
> The old ram turned to the young ram and said, 'I've got an even better idea. Let's walk down the hill and fuck all of the sheep.'

This is the power of living wisdom.

When you honor your inner Mystic, you have access to the Wise Man's counsel when you need it. You can actually develop a relationship with your wisdom where you can sit down, invoke that side of yourself, and ask it important life questions and get answers. Eventually, we want to learn to live from that place of wisdom all the time. But at the very least, we need to know this part of ourselves and have access to it.

Owning our Mystic Power is also about keeping in mind that, as a man, you need to keep learning as you grow older. When we do this, our age becomes a great asset. Traditional societies honor the young men for their Warrior abilities, and honor the old men for their wisdom. Of course, just because we're old doesn't mean we're wise. Plenty of old men are as stupid as anyone else. But if you approach your path with the intention of honoring this inner Mystic Power, your old man's rocking chair becomes your seat of inner power.

The opposite of wisdom is foolishness. We act like fools when we know better but act in an unwise way anyhow. When we look at the stupid things we've done, most of them could have been avoided if we took the time to consider the wisest way. It's not about killing spontaneity or over-thinking everything. It's just learning to have wisdom on your side. It's learning to honor our 'good sense.'

> Owning our Mystic Power is also about keeping in mind that, as a man, you need to keep learning as you grow older.

It's also a good idea for you to take stock of how you take care of your mind. What do you feed it? Do you feed it mental junk food like stupid TV or social media? Or overwhelm it with worthless video games and white noise all the time? Owning your wisdom means that you give a fuck about your mind: you honor your intellect and you respect yourself in this way.

2. THE SHAMAN

Assuming we own our basic good sense, intelligence, and wisdom, we also have another important aspect of the Mystic energy. I call it the Shaman. This is our ability to be 'mystical,' it's our hard-wired ability to get beyond the material world and connect with Spirit. It's what you could call your spiritual intelligence or your mystical heart. This is the part that we use to get the Second Key – a deep and authentic spiritual connection.

Outward and Inward

The Shaman aspect of our Mystic Power is like a mask that faces both outward and inward. The Shaman can bridge out of the ordinary world of time and space and connect with the mysterious powers of the universe. It's also the ability to go inward and connect with your own spirit, with your deep psyche, and with your soul or deep essence. If you are a man of faith, your Shaman aspect is that power that allows your faith to be an experienced thing, not just an intellectual one. If you have your Shaman intact, your prayer is more potent and effective. If you are not religious, even if you are an atheist, this part is still important. If nothing else, the Shaman gives you the ability to crack yourself open, know yourself deeply, and make yourself a better man.

Kumbaya

Because so much modern spirituality is woman focused, many men shy away from this aspect of the Mystic. They call it 'woo-woo' or 'kumbaya.' I think these reactions are because most men just haven't experienced spiritual practice in a masculine context. The ultra-feminine New Age spirituality that we see these days is a very modern development. Most traditional spiritual practices were developed by men for men. If you're in doubt, attend a traditional sweat lodge on my Iroquois buddy's reservation. You'll feel like you're being boiled alive. It's the opposite of kumbaya. It's hardcore. But hardcore in a deeply authentic spiritual way. Bridging from the material world to the spiritual realm is not the action of a weakling. The Shaman's strength is a massive strength.

In our retreats and gatherings, we do regular sitting meditation, but we also mix it up and do meditations with drums, or outdoor meditations sitting around a fire. We go to the woods and connect to the ancient forces of nature. We dig deep into our hearts and minds and share our findings with the other men. No one has to feel like a sissy. The weird feelings come when men try to conform to someone else's idea of spiritual. We go with our wife to the yoga studio and feel out of place. We listen to a popular spiritual celebrity and know in our hearts they're not speaking to us. What we all need to do is to find the sorts of practices that work for us and make them our own. And then work the hell out of them. The Shaman is not a dabbler. The Shaman knows how to go balls-deep into spiritual practice. When we have a strong practice that really works for us, we gain a whole new kind of mojo.

3. THE MEDICINE MAN

The Mystic is not only our wisdom and spiritual power, it is our healing power. The Mystic gives us the power of the Medicine Man. He is our ability to get into our own psyche and heal what needs healing and hone what needs honing. We learn from our dreams. We can meditate on deep questions and receive answers from within. Our Mystic is the part of us that can clean up our Mental Bullshit and help us to get free. When you have your Mystic intact, you can travel back in time and revisit the old wounds and heal them. You can examine your patterns and your conditioning. You can choose more empowering beliefs and put them into practice. You can quieten your mind with meditation and focus your inner power on achieving your purpose and your vision.

The Mystic doesn't have to operate alone. Along with sharing your practice with other men, you can also seek out other healers and healing modalities to enrich your inner process. If you have your own inner Mystic intact, then you won't get swindled and you'll have a gut sense of what really works and what is just 'kumbaya' bullshit. And, honestly, there is a lot of bullshit out there. If you are looking for a meditation teacher, or a healing retreat or the like, you have to shop around and really trust that gut sense.

4. SUPERPOWERS

I once had conversation with an elder of the Winnebago (Ho Chunk) Nation. He described a part of his coming-of-age ceremony. He was told,

> Now you're a man, and as a man, you're expected to fast. You fast so that you can see things without your eyes. You fast so that you can hear things without your ears. You fast so that you can touch things without your hands and know things without your mind.

This is a great description of the work we do to hone our Mystic energy – whether it's sitting meditation, or silent walking, or private moments of prayer. Contemporary physics tells us that the whole universe is made of energy. The Mystic knows this experientially. When our Mystic is intact, we are sensitive to the energy in the world around us. We can sense trouble before it happens, we can know other people's intentions, even if they're hidden. When you're able to get into your own heart and head, you can get

> When our Mystic is intact, we are sensitive to the energy in the world around us.

into the hearts and heads of others, and you can resist it if others are trying to fuck with yours. When you hone your Mystic, you gain psychic strength.

The Mystic gives a man superpowers. In particular I see that men who have an intact spiritual intelligence and regular spiritual practices have three special powers:

- We gain the ability to see and work beneath the surface level of things.
- We gain a clarity in our mind and senses and are able to more deeply appreciate beauty.
- We don't get caught in the bullshit and petty stuff of life.

These may seem like no big deal. But if you really look at them and look into them, you'll see that they are incredible and rare powers for men to have in today's world.

Dirt Time

The practices that we do to get our superpowers may be spiritual or mystical, but it's still work. Like working on an engine or tilling an orchard, we have to put in some effort. I call this spiritual effort 'dirt time.' It's a term I stole from the great tracking master Tom Brown Jr. He uses 'dirt time' to refer to the time a tracker spends down on his belly in the woods, learning the ins and outs of the animal he's tracking, examining tracks, searching for clues, and so on. Our spiritual dirt time is about getting down and looking at our own inner mechanics, it's about tracking our own inner power and inner truth in the jungle of our busy lives, thoughts, desires, and confusions. When it comes to getting free from our inner bullshit, dirt time is an essential component.

Your Inner Land
Just as we all have a physical place to live, like a house or apartment, or physical property measured in square feet, we also each have within us our own inner space. You could think of it as an inner world or your inner land. It's our mind, our consciousness, our emotional self, our emotional storehouse, our mental space. It's a fertile soil, like the richest, most perfect, raw piece of land you can imagine. Everything that we experience in our outer life grows from this inner soil. All of our relationships, projects, life events, and outer situations have their roots in our inner land. Our deep beliefs and feelings create mental reactions and emotions that guide our decisions and actions, which create our outer life. Our spiritual practice time becomes a time where we sit down and engage with that inner ground, our inner soil. This is a revolutionary practice. Many great and successful men throughout history – inventors, leaders, innovators – have attributed their success to a combination of hard outer work with hard inner work. Ask any man who is wildly successful about his inner life. He may or may not do formal meditation or mystical practice, but I promise you he has something that gives him an inner edge.

Tending the Land
How do we tend this inner land? We might choose to have a meditation practice where we sit silently and go into our raw

consciousness. We may choose to have a journaling practice where we examine our choices and write out or draw our vision. Sometimes men have an active prayer practice where they voice their hopes and fears and intentions to Spirit. Whatever we do, we're paying attention to this fertile and super-important dimension of ourselves. We see what may have grown there when we weren't looking: negativities, fears, avoidance patterns, resentments, stupid beliefs, 'mushrooms' in the night. Then we have the chance with our meditation, our prayer, our journal writing, and our visionary practice to get in there and uproot the things we don't want to grow there.

Have something in your life that goes against your grain, something that is way out of line with your vision? Look at the inner soil that it is growing in. There's nothing that we do or choose or experience in our outer life that isn't rooted in our inner world. If you do your dirt time daily or a few times a week, you develop a relationship with this part of yourself and come to know it. It's like a piece of land you tend to every day: you know when there's something off about the soil; you know when there's an imbalance of negativity taking root in that soil. The better you know yourself, the better you can use your spiritual practice to cultivate an energy of positivity – an energy of sacredness and aliveness and power. Cultivate an energy of intentionality. Only grow what you choose in your inner soil. Your inner land is yours.

Pulling Weeds
Just having a regular awareness practice, where you keep track of this side of your self, is a massive shift for many men. Many imbalances and unwanted fungi can't stand the light of our attention. But in some cases, we have deeper healing work to do. Sometimes we need to use our Mystic Power to actively uproot negative energies or patterns.

If you keep a journal and notice that you're bogged down in a resentment or some other negativity, you can come up with specific positive ways of thinking and feeling to replace the unconscious ones. If you feel overwhelmed, you might choose to write out all the things that are overwhelming you and use your inner Warrior to come up with a plan of attack. You might need to battle feelings of depression with vision and positivity and inspiration, or use meditation and conscious down-time to quiet restlessness and anxiety. There is really no one-size-fits-all prescription for this stuff. You need to get in there and see what you need. If you can't manage your inner land alone, get help. Reach out to a mentor or counselor, or join a men's group. Open up to a man in your life and talk things through. Write your highest intentions on a piece of paper and offer it ceremonially to a fire as a form of prayer.

The Way of the Crow

An important aspect of the Mystic is the ability to transform darkness. I call this the Way of the Crow. Every man has a parcel of darkness. Our failures, our fears, our shame, our grief – these things are in us. And if we don't know how to work with them, they can consume us or force us to become numb or dumb – switched off. Every man needs to know how to deal with his darkness and 'keep his devil in the hole.' The Mystic gives us the ability to be fearless and look at our darkness and not be freaked out by it – in fact, we learn to honor it, look deeply into it and transform it into power, into light, into wisdom.

There is a legend about the crow that says that he once was rainbow colored, but he was interested in his shadow and kept staring at it all the time. He looked at it so much that he became the black color of his shadow. If you look at a crow feather in the right light, you can still see the rainbow hues within the black.

The Mystic isn't afraid to look into the black of our life pain, our divorce pain, our bankruptcy pain, and see colors, see wisdom. It gives us the ability to turn our pain and failure into gold.

BRUTAL HONESTY

Without blaming or shaming yourself, make a list of five major failures, breakdowns, or misfortunes that you've experienced in your life. Then examine each one and see:

1. What did you learn from the experience?
2. How did this experience contribute to your personal growth?
3. Looking back, what could have been a wiser approach to that situation? How might a wiser approach have changed the experience for the better?

BAD KARMA

Even if you have the most kick-ass consciousness practice, you're still going to have moments where your inner land is in bad shape. It's very important when you notice this that you don't act from this place. Try not to speak too much from this place. Further actions and speech that come from a bad inner soil will only produce 'bad karma.' Bad karma doesn't mean bad luck or past bad actions coming back to you. Bad karma in the most basic sense just means bad or unwanted results in your outer life: bad responses from other people, bad days, bad weeks, bad years.

It's the same thing with good inner soil. When you know that you've got some really good soil: positivity, groundedness, passion, clarity of vision, and purpose – act! Make choices, speak your Truth, hatch your plans. Good inner soil produces good karma, meaning good results, good days, and a conscious life.

BEST PRACTICES FOR HONING YOUR MYSTIC POWER

So how do we connect with our inner Mystic? How do we nourish our spiritual side without betraying our masculine sensibilities? I will outline a few simple practices that you can integrate into your life, but it's up to you to tweak them and customize them and make them your own.

Study

If we are to grow in wisdom as we grow in years, it's important to keep our learning faculties strong. It's very important for men to keep learning, keep studying. Find books that enrich you and read them. Get audio books for your car or to listen to with your headphones. Find podcasts that stimulate new ideas and challenge your old ones. Travel, not just for entertainment but for the sake of exploring other cultures. Learn new skills. Find something difficult and learn to do it. Find other men who are also on the Red Road and discuss what you're learning or learn something together. Never stop exercising your inner self.

Solitude

Most men need solitude for their mental health and deep happiness. We need to get away from the noise of our lives, and the people that depend on us, to recollect and rejuvenate ourselves.

The kings in ancient times had pleasure gardens where they would go to be by themselves and meditate or contemplate. Think of the typical image of a dad out in the yard by himself, watering the lawn, or tinkering with something in the garage. Yeah, the lawn needed watering and the thing needed tinkering, but the other thing that was happening was dad getting his solitude. You can always mix it up and do inner work with others or in groups, but most need to do the bulk of their contemplative work in solitude.

Make time to be by yourself for the purpose of connecting with yourself. Solitude's not the same as just 'being alone.' It's deliberate. Solitude is a practice. Schedule in moments in your week where you can be by yourself in your own energy field without distraction. This is one of the reasons I cherish my time on my motorcycle. Even if I am riding with friends, the time on two wheels is time with myself and my breathing, and the wind, and the road. Some men like biking, or fishing, or building projects. Play around and experiment for yourself and find your moments of intentional solitude.

Walking

Walking is a great practice for men to get into their Mystic. It's a perfect way to get some solitude, get some exercise, reflect on your purpose, and connect to Spirit, all in one. Walking can be a simple walk around the block, or a regular 'constitutional' that we do every day. Walking is a great way to blow off steam if you have pent-up energy. It's also a good way to stay connected to the outdoors. I walk all year round, including in the winter when it's freezing outside. Men who live in cold climates can get sedentary in the winter and spend all their time indoors. Many mornings I walk the two miles from my home to my office. It gives time to reflect on my vision for the day and get my blood pumping. It prepares me for my day in a way that riding my motorcycle or taking a cab doesn't. If I walk hard I get to work pumped and feeling good, even if there are icicles in my beard. I could include the walking practice in any of these chapters. It's good for the Warrior, King, and Lover in us too. I'm putting it here because I find it first and foremost a Mystic's practice to walk. Many of my best insights happen on foot.

If you want, you can also try doing what I call a Spirit Walk. It's a kind of walking meditation. It's a more deliberate spiritual practice. When I Spirit Walk, I have no other purpose for the walk. I'm not trying to get somewhere. Usually, when I Spirit Walk, I move a little slower. I like to Spirit Walk in nature, on the beach or in the woods or desert, but it can be really cool to do it in the city as well. When I do it, I keep my eyes in soft focus, taking in everything around me. All of my senses are wide open and I'm aware of my body and my breathing. I take time to notice everything, feel the energy where I'm walking, smell the air, absorb the power of the natural place. There are other traditional kinds of walking meditation you can learn. At Tom Brown Jr's tracker school I learned a powerful kind of stalking he calls 'fox walking.' It's a silent, super-slow-motion walk that he learned from his Apache scout master, where you become hyper-aware of everything around you, and you're virtually invisible.

The simplest way to try walking as a spiritual practice is simply to take the time to go somewhere, put your phone away, and walk. Clearing your head, connecting to your spirit, step by step. Try it.

Find your Soul Place(s)

Do you have a power spot, a soul place that is where you love to go to do your inner work? A soul place is a place where you can more easily access your Mystic. It can be a spot that you can

> A soul place is a place where you can more easily access your Mystic.

drive to and park your car, or an outdoor place where you love to walk or sit. Of course your soul place can be in your house, too. I know many men who have a room set aside just for reflection, spiritual, and creative work. Some men use their workshops or dens or garages as soul places. It's good to have a few.

I have a special spot in Brooklyn, across the East River from where we live in Manhattan. I like to take the short ride over the bridge on my motorcycle and park by the water. It's directly across from where our apartment is; I can see the buildings of our complex, but they're a half-mile away across the river. I love to sit by the lapping water and enjoy that half-mile of distance for perspective. Many great decisions and deep prayers have been made from that spot. I try to find soul places wherever I travel, in walking distance from my hotel, or near where I'm teaching. Often times I'll find good soul places on rooftops of buildings.

Along with the spots I have in my day-to-day life, I also have special spots that I have visited around the world. Sometimes you find these places and sometimes they find you. There's a sacred mountain in India, for instance, that I absolutely love. It's silent and ancient and feels super holy. It's in a remote place, so I don't visit there often, but I make a point to go there when I can. As a contrast, there is a tea shop in the incredibly busy city of Mumbai that holds a similar place in my heart. It's loud and chaotic, but I love to sit there and sip tea and write in my journal. Another place like that for me is Gorongosa National Park in Mozambique. I've only been there a couple of times, but those visits are burned into my heart. All I have to do is remember my times in that African wilderness – the lions, the landscape, the smell of the grasslands – and I connect deeply with the spirit of the place. Try taking a soul vacation – travel somewhere not for 'entertainment' but specifically as a pilgrimage. Go there to cultivate a soul connection with a place.

Nature

The Mystic has a particular connection to nature. The Mystic goes into nature and treats it as a temple, as a place of worship. The Mystic in us loves the solitude of nature and the purity of the elements. The Mystic in us loves to sit staring at a campfire. It loves the sound of thunder. I would have to say that being in nature is my personal favorite foolproof spiritual practice. Wild things are living in total harmony with each other, and living their truth 100 per cent. When we're in a wilderness or natural place, we are in the energy field of this dynamic harmony. We can learn so many spiritual lessons by hanging out with a tree, or a deer, or even a sky full of clouds. Next time you're freaking out or feeling out of sorts, try getting outside and finding any wild thing, even if it's just the sky. Clear away your distractions and really connect with whatever it is. Feel your breath and imagine breathing with the wild thing – breathing with the tree, or the storm, or the lake. See if you can get yourself on the same wavelength. Maybe this is why pet owners are said to have longer life expectancy. We get a hit of the wild – even in the form of a silly little dog.

Prayer

You don't have to be a Christian or a Muslim or Jew to pray. You don't need any organized religious tradition. Prayer is simply a conscious connection with whatever is your 'higher power.' In the 12 steps of Alcoholics Anonymous they have an eleventh step that reads:

The Mystic

We sought through prayer and meditation to improve our conscious contact with God as we understood Him, praying only for knowledge of His will for us and the power to carry that out.

I am as non-religious as it gets, but I pray all the time. I try to keep my conscious contact constant. I will often pray as I walk, or as I ride my motorcycle. I pray when I'm falling asleep and when I wake. I pray when I need support and when I feel fear. Sometimes I pray out loud. I don't even think about who I am praying to. It's more like I'm praying to a force – the force that holds and supports and creates everything. Most of my prayers are informal, but I have a few set prayers that I have memorized and use in important moments. One that I use daily comes again from AA. It's a variation of the third-step prayer.

God I offer myself to you.
To build with me and do with me as You will.
Take away the bondage of myself that I may better do
Your will.
Take away my difficulties, that I may bear witness to
Your Power, Your Love, and Your Way of Life.
May I always do Your will.

The language is kind of old fashioned, but I find it very powerful. A core part of my purpose is service, so this is a great prayer to realign me and connect me to what's important. For more than a quarter-century, this prayer has been a daily part of my life.

Play around with prayer. Try using your own simple informal prayers or try more traditional ones if you feel a connection to them. See what happens.

Sitting Meditation

Another very effective practice you can do is a simple sitting meditation practice. There are hundreds of meditation techniques to choose from. In meditation, you clear away outer distractions and focus solely on your inner self. I think some meditation – even if it's just a few minutes every day – is an essential practice for men. Don't worry about making your mind shut up – it won't. Just sit and give it space. Connect to your deeper energies, your heart energies, your 'deep masculine' power. Connect to your inner Warrior. Sit and remember all the things you're grateful for. There are many, many ways to do it. The important thing is to find something you enjoy – and feel free to adapt it. Many meditations come from spiritual and religious traditions, so often there's religious baggage tied the practice. You'll read that a certain practice is the only true meditation technique, or that in order to meditate you must do 'X, Y, Z, ...' – that sort of thing. It's all bullshit.

> I think some meditation – even if it's just a few minutes every day – is an essential practice for men.

Meditating is like sleeping – it's a process where you put yourself into an alternative state of consciousness. It's your practice, and your consciousness. You can do it any way that works for you and gets you the result you want. You could also consider learning some *pranayamas* – yogic breathing techniques – to add to your meditation regime.

Breath Work

Breathing techniques can be great helpers when it comes to meditation, but they are also fine practices on their own. There's a deep connection between the breath and the mind. If you don't believe me, notice your breathing the next time you're agitated. Learning to take command of your breathing and altering it is a powerful way to bring some discipline to your mind and emotions. Different kinds of breathing produce different results. You can breathe intensely to pump yourself up, or breathe calmly to cool yourself down. The most basic things you can do are just stop holding your breath, start noticing your breath, and breathe more consciously.

SIMPLE BREATHING EXERCISE

Sit comfortably with your feet flat on the floor. Close your eyes and count off 3 slow, long breaths in and out through your nose. When you breathe in, imagine gathering up all of your mental stress and physical exhaustion. When you breathe out, imagine letting it all go like exhaust. After the 3 long breaths, breathe naturally for a few rounds and notice how you feel. Repeat the sets of 3 long breaths as many times as you need to to shift your state of mind and body.

BRUTAL HONESTY

What's Your Bullshit About the Mystic?

Do you consider yourself intelligent or stupid?

How do you relate to other men who are considered

wise or spiritual or evolved? What's your general feeling about spiritual matters? Do you have a relationship to a 'higher power'? Does spiritual talk make you uncomfortable? What, if anything, is preventing you from enriching your spiritual life or enhancing your power of wisdom?

Learn How to Just Be

A man with backbone needs to know how to just be: just sitting there, or standing there, or being there without needing to constantly do something, fidget with something, or stimulate himself. These days, with all of the electronic media available, we can avoid being with ourselves. Every potentially quiet moment can be filled with text messaging or checking our smart phones. Sudoku, crossword puzzles, video games, empty talk radio – the list of mindless distractions and time passers could go on and on. Just be. If you can learn to just sit, just be with yourself quietly for a moment, you will be a more powerful, free and deep man. In some ways, this is the hardest practice.

Try these or anything else to strengthen your Mystic. Remember to make them your own. Remember trial and error – experiment. Let go of what doesn't work and do more of what does. It's the best way to make it real and make sure what you're doing is authentic and effective. Bottom line: *do something*. Honor your inner Mystic and learn to nourish it in a way that really works for you on your terms.

SUMMING UP THE MYSTIC

The Mystic – is a man's power of consciousness, wisdom, and spirit. The Mystic has three main aspects:
> **The Wise Man** – the power of living wisdom, good sense, and intelligence
>
> **The Shaman** – our spiritual intelligence
>
> **The Medicine Man** – the power to heal inner wounds and gain mystical powers.

The Mystic gives a man power to see beneath the surface level of things, clarity of the mind and senses, and freedom from the bullshit and petty stuff of life.

Every man needs to hone and honor his consciousness through learning, disciplined spiritual practice, and inner healing.

INVEST IN YOUR MYSTIC

Put this into practice. Create a customized Mystic practice regime for yourself. See what kind of practices appeal to you. Learn to meditate. Start keeping a journal. Choose any of the practices suggested in this chapter or any others that attract you. Let it be a process of trial and error.

11

THE LOVER

aving backbone isn't all about being strong and brutal and
serious; it's about being open and loving too. The Lover is our
power to enjoy our life. It is the part of us that loves and is able to
be loved. It's our masculine sensitivity to beauty and our ability to
relate to romantic partners, to have a robust and enjoyable sex life.
The Lover sits across from the Warrior. The Warrior is the part of us
that is about getting stuff done and hardens us when we need to be
firm. The Lover is the part that opens up and lets the guard down to
just be, enjoy pleasure, and connect with the world around us.

If your Lover Power is intact and in balance, you will hold the
key to loving three essential things: life, sex, and the beauty of
everything.

Although it is the 'softest' of the Four Powers, it is in many
ways the most important because it insures that we attain the
Three Keys. The Lover makes sure that our vision and purpose are
not just wise, but enjoyable. It helps us to not get too serious or
rigid in our spiritual practice, and gives us the ability to vision a

beautiful, bullshit-free existence. Instead of a Red Road walking away from the bad, the Lover helps us forge a shining Red Path to the best in ourselves and in life.

1. THE LOVER LOVES

Thawing Out

Too many of us are frozen. Getting the Lover means thawing out our ability to be open to the full experience of life. It means waking up our senses to appreciate all kinds of beauty and pleasure. It's about defrosting our emotional body so that we can feel deeply and express our feelings when we need to. Too many men live solely in their heads, all but cut off from their hearts. Black Road men allow themselves basically two feelings: anger and lust. On the Red Road we need to reclaim and enjoy the full spectrum of human emotions. This includes enthusiasm. If a corny sitcom on TV wants to depict a gay or effeminate man, it will usually make him super enthusiastic, as if to say that enthusiasm is un-masculine. The word 'enthusiasm' literally means to be filled with Spirit. We get our Lover when we allow ourselves to belly up to the bar of life with great enthusiasm and order *everything*.

Thawing out and getting our Lover means allowing ourselves to feel, to laugh, to play, to dance – to be fully alive. It's the completing piece of the Four Powers model. Without the Lover the King is too serious, the Warrior is too brutal, the Mystic is too dry. The Lover gives us access to the spice of life.

Russell the Love Muscle

It might be obvious, but a big part of the Lover energy is the power to love and be loved. I call this power 'Russell the Love Muscle.'

I experience it like an actual muscle or power center in me that feels love. In many men, this muscle is weak or frozen. We may 'know' that we love something or someone. We might declare our love or demonstrate it with action. But do we really feel love?

Like enthusiasm or spirituality, love as a feeling is something more associated with the feminine realm. As men, we have a huge capacity for love. But our love is different. It comes with a dose of wanting to serve, a protective Papa Bear energy. Men are very nurturing too, but it's a masculine nurturing energy. If we allow ourselves to feel this nurturing energy, the Lover Power will be more accessible for us. It's not about becoming feminine or soft, it's about waking up our deep masculine loving heart and setting it loose on our world. Start noticing your love muscle. Pay attention to what makes it flex; exercise it. Honor your masculine Papa Bear love and start to see areas of your life that need it.

As we awaken our Lover, we also need to pay attention to our need for love. We feel this in the 'love muscle' too. The Lover needs to love, but he also needs to be held, needs to be stroked, and taken care of. This aspect of the Lover is a tough one for many men to open up to. It is vulnerability. Some men can only access their softness after sex.

Making ourselves vulnerable can be scary. We might feel that if we open this dimension of our heart, we might be rejected, hurt, and disappointed. Some of us have painful experiences in our past that have caused us to put up walls around our hearts. These walls are for the Black Road. On the Red Road, we learn how to own and operate our hearts and use the heart's power. Russell the Love Muscle becomes our good friend. Yes, we can get hurt when our heart is open. But we have our King's vision, our Warrior's boundaries, and the Mystic's wisdom to protect us and allow us to love hard.

> **BRUTAL HONESTY**
> How strong is your love muscle? What do you love?
> Who do you love? In what areas of your life is it
> easy to love? Where is it hard?

2. SEX

Sex is not the only aspect of the Lover energy, but it's a big one and one that too many men get hung up on. So let's go there. Our sex energy, like our violent energy, is something that is hard-wired and very strong in men. It doesn't matter if you are a poon-chasing stud or a feminist, celibate priest – if you're a man, you have a volcanic sex drive and a basic orientation toward sexual thinking and sexual desire. A man on his Red Road needs to truly own his sexual power and learn how to operate it the same way he does his inner Warrior qualities.

It's funny: men are so sex oriented – even sex obsessed – and yet this is still an area that needs a huge amount of work. There are many reasons why men get hung up in the sex arena. First, there's a kind of societal thing that keeps our 'sexy beast' under wraps. The stereotype for an un-evolved man has him wanting to hump anything that moves. There is some truth to this. Men with healthy libidos do have a ton of sexual wanting. But it's just not okay to express sexual desire openly in the office, on the bus, on the street. It's not a big secret that society, especially in the US, is very

> A man on his Red Road needs to truly own his sexual power and learn how to operate it the same way he does his inner Warrior qualities.

schizophrenic about sex. On the one hand it's obsessed with sex: there is sex everywhere – pictures of sexy people on every ad, and sexual stuff all over the place. On the other hand, we still have our puritanical repressed shame about sex and have a very hard time being open about our actual sexual behaviors.

Men walk around thinking about and wanting sex all the time, and most of the time we have to pretend that that's not what we're thinking or wanting. I read somewhere that men think about sex 10 times every minute that they are awake. Assuming this is true, how do we make that work for us instead of against us? And how do we shine the light of awareness on our sexuality in a way that makes us more powerful, rather than less powerful?

Primal Desire

For most men, on some level, we want sex with anyone who we find attractive. It doesn't matter if we are in a relationship or not. It doesn't matter if the situation is appropriate or not. Baba Ram Dass, the great spiritual teacher, once honestly described his sexual mind walking down the street in New York City – filing everyone who passed into one of three categories: potential, competition, or irrelevant. That's just how it is. It's a primal desire that is not about our choices in life, or our vision, or what we consider appropriate or wise. Look at all of the great men who have been brought down when they acted on their wanting. The Mystic in us is often sidelined when the Lover is in its primal desire mode, but you can see how the wise counsel of your Mystic is important here.

It is very liberating if we can just let ourselves off the hook for looking. We look at butts, we look at crotches. We look at breasts,[1]

---

1   Here, because I am heterosexual, I am using female examples. If you're gay, you can just apply the same ideas to desire for sex with men. Thing is, if you're gay, you've probably worked through a lot of this already.

we imagine having sex with waitresses while they are taking our orders. A beautiful woman talks to us and our mind drifts to imagine our cock in her mouth. It doesn't matter who they are. If they are young and attractive, we do the same thing with nuns when we see them in their habits. As we move through the world, we undress women with our eyes and are semi-constantly on the look-out for viable sex partners.

This sort of looking, this desire-driven relating has nothing to do with our respect for women or our fidelity to our committed relationships. It's a beautiful, wild part of us. Of course I am not suggesting that we follow this part of ourselves, or make our life choices accordingly, or act out our fantasies with the waitresses or nuns. I'm just suggesting that we don't deny our feelings, or pretend they're not happening, or shame ourselves for having them. These energies get us in trouble when we try to deny them and let them fester in the shadows. We want to be good citizens and not harass women by staring or construction-site hooting and whistling, but there is something really liberating about letting ourselves gaze, letting ourselves appreciate women's beauty, and allowing ourselves to feel the arousal and sexual interest.

When you get your Lover intact, along with the King, Warrior, and Mystic, you don't have to be afraid of yourself or your impulses. Your Lover becomes a really enjoyable part of yourself.

Don't Put the Poontang on a Pedestal

One evening, as I rode my motorcycle into the city for a men's group, I saw my mind do something. It was a warm summer evening and the streets were teaming with people. But I didn't see any men. Nor did I see any old women – or children. I only saw attractive women of child-bearing age. All over the place. It wasn't that the other people actually weren't there; it was that my mind had tuned them out and only saw the potential sex partners. We had a very rich discussion in our group that night about 'pussy' and its hold on us.

Allow me to get a little 'Robert Bly' for a minute: As boys, we weren't given any ritual initiation into manhood. We weren't taken out into the woods and given a spiritual experience. We weren't taken into a sweat lodge to have a divine vision. There wasn't a moment when we were taken away by the old men in our community, trained, and blessed into manhood. Most of us 'became men' the first time we got into a girl's pants. Or at least that experience was the most profound experience we had had up to that point in life. It was the closest thing to a spiritual experience; it blew us away and changed us forever. And from that point on, that pussy, that principle, that access to a female's most vulnerable power spot and the accompanying attention – became our holy grail. We don't necessarily remember the times our fathers or grandfathers taught us about life, but every man remembers the first time he fingered a girl. We've lost interest in the opinions of other men, and our good standing with other men; by and large, we've become obsessed with our ability to get laid and get the loving attention of females. If we are to transition from the Black Road to the Red, we need to rearrange this.

When we are unconscious, we will lie for pussy; we will die for pussy. We will betray our best friends and loved ones for the sake of it. Great men of every generation have been brought down by their fascination with it. We follow it into and out of marriages, and make all kinds of life decisions consciously or unconsciously for the sake of having proximity and access to it. This is true for the sexually active among us, and it is just as true for men who never get to have sex. It's mostly a mental motivational thing. This changes a little bit as men get older. But just a little bit. I once had an older cab driver tell me, 'The day

I realized I was old was the day I realized I would rather have a good dump than a good lay.'

A huge step that every man can take is to just own up to this, recognize his love for it and his desire for it, and then put it in its place. Like everything else in our toolbox, our sexuality and our sexual desire need to be in service to our vision and purpose, instead of vice versa. Within our own psyche, in our own private inner wilderness, we can be unchained, heavy-breathing sexual beasts. But we can also learn how to keep this desire in check. We can find ways to have the excellent sex life that fits with our vision and fulfills us deeply, and then we can take care of the business that we need to take care of. When we have our sexual desire and relationship to it in check, it opens up a whole new world full of all kinds of totally unfuckable people. When we honor and master this aspect of the Lover we can stop deifying women and allow them to simply be women – we can see them as vulnerable human creatures just like us.

> **BRUTAL HONESTY**
> What is your relationship to sex and female attention in general? Have you engaged in dishonorable behavior for the sake of sex?

Porn

These days, porn is a huge thing. In 2012 the US porn industry was estimated at around $8–10 billion. When we were kids in the 1970s and 1980s, porn meant beaver magazines, *Playboy*, and occasionally some XXX videos. You needed a great deal of privacy to watch a VHS movie, and often you had to go rent the thing in a store. Now the internet has made porn totally available and its consumption pretty much anonymous. Also, you can get whatever you want. Any fetish, any particular style of virtual sex is available at the end of a few clicks. Many men, if not most men, these days have some kind of relationship with pornography. Of course, there's nothing 'wrong' with masturbating with porn, but like the other topics here we want to shed some light on it and see what it's doing for us and what it might be taking from us.

There's an argument that porn can be detrimental to our actual sex life. For one thing, it's just not real. Some porn is more real than others, but at the end of the day we are getting aroused and vicariously getting off on a fake thing. The sex is often much more extreme than the sex we're having, and it's lit with professional lights, and usually involves giant cocks on men who are in much better shape than we are. So there is likely some kind of self-esteem issue brewing there too, similar to the kind of thing that happens to girls who are always looking at glamour magazines and comparing themselves to the supermodels in the fashion industry. And then there is the pure training aspect to it too. Usually a man isn't exactly taking his time with a porn video. Often times the videos online are just short, hardcore vignettes. We watch the most potent thing we can find, to get in, get off, and get out. So every time we quickly 'rub one out,' we're training ourselves to orgasm as fast as we can. This isn't exactly elite training for a superior Lover. Men who really indulge heavily in porn even report an inability to get hard or orgasm without it. What we're really hungry for can't be gotten with an online subscription.

The other thing is that most porn is very fuck-and-suck oriented. You don't see many porn stars kissing passionately for a long time, or goof-around cuddling, or taking time to worship each other's bodies slowly and carefully. We have many more erogenous zones than just our cocks and balls. Porn is not going to take time to teach you about any of that. And anyway, even the fucking and sucking is usually fake in porn movies. The actors are using positions and angles that are designed for the camera. Really good sex doesn't look very good on camera. The kind of penetration or oral stimulation that makes a woman orgasm deeply is not the sort of thing most pornos like to show. These days kids are learning how to have sex online. That's like learning to drive by watching choreographed car chase scenes on network TV.

Aside from all that, and the bad training it might be giving us, if there is a key problem with our consumption of porn, it's the same problem that many modern people face in other areas of their lives: we live more in our heads than we do in our bodies. We let the porn stars do all the fucking for us.

If you do enjoy porn I offer you this question: how does the sex you're having in real life compare to the porn you're enjoying online? Is there anything you can learn from the porn that can help you in your real sex life? Because of the vast array of things available online, porn can be a useful way to discover what turns us on, or it can give us a supplement of erotic flavors we just can't get in real life for whatever reason. But beware of porn becoming an out-and-out substitute for a sex life. One of my favorite Zen sayings goes:

Painted cakes do not satisfy hunger.

Real Sex

Along with the vast amount of sex that takes place in our minds and on the internet, if we're lucky, there is also some sex actually happening for us in real life. This is another area I find is underdeveloped in men. We know we want it, we know we love it when it happens, but we seldom take the time to make it excellent or really explore our sexual boundaries.

It's relatively easy for men to get off. Most of us don't need special fantasies or sex positions to have an orgasm. Most of us can do it anytime, anywhere. Unlike women, we don't need to have a partner with any particular skill to get us off in the most basic sense. We can fuck almost anything and achieve climax. (And most men have to stop after one orgasm.) Because of this, many men get lazy and uncreative when it comes to lovemaking with partners.

Let's look at laziness first. I believe it is our duty as men to be skilled at lovemaking. We should be able to make women come and please them in a variety of ways. With a little practice, intention, and discipline, we can learn to hold off our orgasm and 'last longer.' Most women need more stimulation time than we do to have their own climax. It's also true that many women have a hard time orgasming during intercourse and need to be stroked or kissed in a particular way to get off. It's

> Many men get lazy and uncreative when it comes to lovemaking with partners.

worth it to go out of our way to learn these skills and be able to deeply satisfy our partners sexually. Learn how to be a better kisser. Learn how to give good massages, not just so you get more sex, but for the sake of strengthening your inner Lover.

Men need to be more creative sexually too. It's really good for men to explore their sexuality. What really turns you on? What are your fantasies? Aside from your cock, do you know what the 'erogenous zones' of your body are? We don't need to know any of this to get off in the most basic way. I'm talking about taking your lovemaking to the next level. If you take the time to explore yourself and slow down in the kinetic sexual moment, you can learn to wake up your entire body to the lovemaking experience. Then it's not just about your cock and balls: then you're experiencing sex in every cell. With more indepth training, men can even train themselves to have multiple orgasms or at the very least greatly prolong the length of their orgasms.

Sex on the Red Road

It's like anything else on the Red Road. If we are living our life with backbone, we're charged with the task of making our sexuality conscious and in line with our vision. This means giving yourself a break for being sexual in the first place, and then looking at the different parts of your sex life and making them the way you want them to be and striving for a kind of excellence in that area of your life. The Lover is not a humper. The Lover experiences sex as a sacred rite.

A huge shift is when we go from a 'what am I getting' point of view, to a 'what am I giving' point of view. Little boys and guys are always hoping to 'get some.' A man with backbone is aware of who he is and what he brings to the table, and he carries himself accordingly.

Jizz

I have to share something here that I learned in my yoga days. Our sexual fluid – aka our jizz – is really powerful stuff. Not only can it make a baby, it also is full of vital energy. If you come too much too often it will deplete you physically and mentally. In ancient India, young students were advised to be celibate and not to masturbate while they were studying, to keep their minds sharp. It wasn't a moralistic, 'sex is bad' thing. The celibacy rule came from an understanding in Ayurvedic medicine that the semen holds lots of what is called *ojas*. During my years of intense spiritual training, I practiced something called *brahmacharya*: I was totally celibate, avoided masturbating, and even took measures to avoid wet dreams for about three years. It wasn't easy, but it gave me superpowers. It was much easier to meditate, and it gave me a tremendous amount of inner strength.

Some football coaches or military commanders know the same principle and advise their boys to abstain from having sex or jacking off before a game or battle. Pay attention to this dynamic for yourself. If you're coming a lot and find you're getting depleted, try eating foods like almonds, whole milk, bone marrow, and sweet foods like dates or ice cream. These foods help your body to build that ojas back up if you're letting too much of it go.

BRUTAL HONESTY

Are you a good lover? Without shaming yourself in any way, do an honest assessment of your level of mastery as a sex partner. If you're really fearless, ask your most recent partner for a brutally honest performance review. What are some ways that you could improve upon your skill as a lover?

Sex is not the only way that we express our sexuality. The Lover loves sex, and physical pleasure, and human loving, but equally loves any kind of deep connecting. One of the ways that I advise men to break their poontang trance is to learn how to connect to the feminine energies of the universe. Get into the feminine power of nature. Get into the wind, the stars, the woods, the ocean. There's a deep part of us that gets fed when we allow ourselves to connect with the universe in this way. That Lover part of us doesn't just want to enjoy women, it wants to enjoy our food and enjoy our work and enjoy good architecture and enjoy the beauties of the natural world. There is only so much female pleasure allotted to a man. There is a great freedom when we learn how to get that part of us fed by sources that are less costly than women.

3. MASCULINE BEAUTY

The Lover is the part of us that enjoys beauty. Like our spiritual intelligence, this is a power we often give away to the women in our lives. The very word beauty has a feminine connotation, but it doesn't have to. If your Lover is intact, you can have a really clear sense of what you find beautiful or aesthetically appealing. This goes for our appearance, our clothing, the way we maintain our car, and the way we take care of our home.

Whether it's the craftsmanship in a fine piece of woodwork, the unique flavor of a fine whiskey, or the beauty and grace of a master machine like a car or motorcycle, when men are truly present and savoring the sweetness of something beautiful, they are getting their Lover.

Men also hone their Lover when they really take the time to appreciate art. Art means fine art like visual art and sculpture, but it also includes film, music, even quality television shows. There's a difference between zoning out and filling your head with garbage watching some stupid TV show, and really taking the time to choose and enjoy quality content with good writing, acting, and cinematography. Same thing goes for music. Find out what it is for you. Whatever your favorite music is, try listening to it loud with some headphones, without distraction. Really get into it and discover what turns you on about it. It doesn't matter if it's Mozart, Hank Williams, or Slayer. The Lover loves what he loves, but he wants to love it hard.

Grooming

The Lover is the part of us that pays attention to things like grooming. Do you care about your hair? Your clothes? Do you take care of your skin? In my father's day, men would comb their hair and wear pressed clothes every day. It was a regular ritual for men to go to a good barber and get a full treatment, including a shave. You'll find some instances of this in the metrosexual enclaves of the big cities, but most of us modern straight men tend to be slobs. We don't take care of our skin, or keep our nails trimmed and clean. We don't care about how we smell or if our nose hairs are hanging out. All of these things are noticed by women. But even if they don't notice, we should. It's not a matter of being pretty, it's a matter of self-respect and consciousness. On the Red Road a man is aware of what he does and doesn't do. If you choose to have dry, flaky skin and long ear hair, and that serves your purpose and vision – more power to you! But most of us, if we pay attention, can find room for improvement in our grooming department. There's something very energizing about tuning this aspect of our manhood. It isn't about any traditional idea of being well groomed. In my dad's day that meant clean shaven with short hair. I'm talking about taking care of your grooming whatever style you choose.

More on Being Slobs

When you get your Lover on board, you will not only wear better socks, you'll stop leaving them on the floor. You will learn to clean up the toilet after you use it, and also pay attention to the smells your leave around the house. It doesn't matter if you live alone, or if you're dating, or part of a family. Guys are notorious for being pigs when it comes to these things. Women are utterly turned off by a man-aged boy who talks with his mouth full or leaves piss on the bathroom floor. In general, let's have some self-respect and, once again, look at what we do and how we do it. The Warrior can live in a foxhole and shit in a bucket. The Lover is the part of us that can improve our surroundings for us and everyone we share our life with.

This kind of awareness can extend beyond our domestic habits and hygiene and include the way we maintain our vehicles, our lawns, our storage spaces – basically whatever is ours to maintain. The Lover in us loves to get into our brand-new beautiful car and smell the leather seats and enjoy the clean, uncluttered newness. Where does he go months later when there's dust on the dash and all kinds of crap in the folds of the seats? If we take care of our environments and really make it our mission to not be slobs, something in us wakes up. That something is the Lover.

BRUTAL HONESTY

What do you deeply enjoy? Be specific. What music, what food, what art do you deeply love? What can you do to enhance the enjoyment factor in your life? Make a list.

What people, places, and things in your life do you find to be beautiful? Why? Make a list of them and write a few words about each one.

Look at your grooming and the way you present yourself. Are there ways that you can take better care of your appearance? Are there ways in which you're a slob? Are there other areas of your life or living environment that need beautification?

SUMMING UP THE LOVER

The Lover – our power to enjoy life. It is the part of us that feels love and other emotions. It's the part of us that can get goosebumps when we hear a great piece of music. It's the part of us that wants to build things for a woman that we love.

Sex – a strong man needs to really own his sexual power and learn how to operate it the same way he does his inner Warrior qualities.

Women – when we learn to access feminine beauty in nature and in other ways, we can stop deifying women and chasing them for sex and attention.

Masculine Beauty – the Lover is the part of us that enjoys all kinds of beauty. This includes the way we dress and present ourselves, and the way we take care of our homes and possessions.

```
LOVE MUSCLE MEDITATION

Sit quietly with your eyes closed. Take
a moment to think of something, someone,
or somewhere that you really love. Choose
something that you love in an uncomplicated
way. It can be a pet, a favorite place, or a
child – whatever really makes you feel the
love. Then, just focus on the feeling. Notice
where you feel it in your body and breathe
into that part. See how hard you can love. See
if you can love so hard you make yourself cry.
```

Part Three

PUTTING IT ALL INTO PRACTICE

Now that you've learned about the Three Keys and Four Powers, the question is – what do you do with all this knowledge? I believe the knowledge is a burden if we don't act on it. The purpose of the work that I do with men – that this book is an expression of – is to make lives better. In this third and final section, we will discuss what it means to live with this knowledge – how to bring your backbone out into your world.

12

INNER ENEMIES

Few of us really have to fight people today. Unless we're a soldier or a cop, chances are that we rarely, if ever, have to get involved in actual physical violence. That doesn't mean we don't have enemies. We absolutely do. We have formidable enemies in the form of our own bad habits and Mental Bullshit. Our enemies are inside of our own head: self-hatred, laziness, fear, anger, insensitivity, distraction, lack of grit, prejudice, pessimism, resentments, self-absorption, addiction, meanness, gullibility, dishonesty, arrogance, stupidity, greed, disrespect, depression, anxiety, worrying, sloth, lack of discipline ... the list could go on and on. All of these things are enemies. Why? Because they are the enemies of our vision. They are the enemies of the King. If any of the enemies from the list above really takes you over, your mission to find your backbone and attain the Three Keys will fail, without doubt.

The combat warrior trains and makes his body strong and hones his martial skill. The man in possession of a strong inner Warrior needs to make his heart strong and hone the skill of detecting and fighting these inner enemies. It's our Warrior's job to protect our life from these.

Without some conscious work, it is common for men to fall prey to certain 'inner enemies' or qualities of being that don't support us living in our bigness. If there is any good use for our inner Warrior, it is to battle these foes. We don't choose them; they grow like weeds when the Mystic isn't tending our inner land. You'll relate more to some of the enemies than to others. Some men have been defeated and made slaves to these enemies. A man on the Black Road is most prone to them. But all men – even the most conscious among us – will find these enemies lurking within us, ready to attack us in our weaker moments.

We could make a massive list of possible enemies – and ultimately you will have to figure out your own – but the most dangerous ones are passivity, immaturity, cowardice, callousness, distraction, anger, and self-emasculation.

PASSIVITY

One of the main ailments that men today suffer from is passivity. If the Red Road requires us to live with backbone, the Black Road requires a man to be shrunken, without his Four Powers. As a species, the modern man has been de-balled. Our inner guard dog has been muzzled. Our inner Warrior has been disarmed. The passive man is prone to his inner enemies and prone to the other challenges in his life. I choose this word prone on purpose. It means lying down. Challenges arise, enemies attack, and the passive part of us lies down.

> The passive man is prone to his inner enemies and prone to the other challenges in his life.

Sometimes when we think of a passive man, we think of a 'wimpy guy.' Surely there is plenty of wimpyness in the modern man. This is what one of my biker friends, Grizz, refers to as the 'general pussification' of modern men. We don't use tools, we can't bear pain, we don't know how to stand up for ourselves or what we believe in. This is all generally true, but the kind of passivity I am talking about is a little more subtle.

Some of us do become 'pushovers' or 'spineless pussies' if we are passive to the extreme, but often it's more about an overly mild, non-assertive approach to life. The passive man drifts through life and lets life tell him how to be and what to do. He's overly controlled by others' expectations of him. The man on the Black Road is owned by his life, by his job, by his debt, by his family duties. He does the bare minimum of what he has to do to stay out of trouble and avoids situations where he has to stand up for himself. This passive man lacks grit, he lacks the Warrior qualities he needs to kick ass and make changes in life. A passive man can sleepwalk through life. His wife, his boss, his kids, and his habits will tell him what to do and when to do it.

When we're being passive, we're not just passive with life, we're passive with ourselves as well. A man without backbone doesn't know himself deeply – although he may do lots of self-help workshops or therapy. A passive man doesn't know himself deeply because he doesn't live deeply. As men, looking at ourselves in meditation rooms or therapists' offices isn't enough; we need to live hard into our life and know ourselves by testing ourselves against the world. When we are passive, we rob ourselves of crucial self-knowledge.

When we're passive, we get pushed around by the women in our life. We get led around like a leashed animal, chasing their affection or approval. This includes access to 'physical affection' – aka poontang. When we're passive we often cut ourselves off from other men. We're afraid of and avoid strong men or big men. When we're passive, we seek out people, places, and situations that make us comfortable with our smallness. A deeply happy, powerful man is oriented around a sense of bigness. When we've succumbed to our passivity our center of gravity is the opposite: smallness and pettiness.

You'd think that passivity would make a man harmless, but it's the opposite. When we go into passivity, we become really dangerous. We might not yell, or fight or threaten. We may not beat our kids or dominate our women, but that doesn't mean we're harmless. When we're passive, we harm with our passivity. We harm our women by not committing, and not making choices, and not holding the masculine energy in the relationship. We force our women to make all the hard choices and 'wear the pants' in our relationship. When we're passive we harm our children by not being whole, by not living with passion and vision and teaching our children what a powerful man is. Sons raised by passive men won't learn to take themselves seriously. If we father our sons in this way, we'll inadvertently teach them how to be dominated by women, how to hide out, and how to be enslaved by life.

Antidotes to Passivity

The greatest antidote to passivity lies within the First Key. Passivity gets the best of us when we don't have a clear vision or know our purpose. This means our big vision and purpose for our life, but also the vision and purpose for a specific moment. You can practice this the next time you go out to eat. Get crystal clear why you are eating where you're eating and choose and eat your food very deliberately. Try it. It's so simple but it will show you something. Then apply this to all areas of your life – your relationships, your work, your role in society – you'll see.

IMMATURITY

Way too many men today are immature in a certain way. When we're immature instead of being men, we're just 'guys.' A guy is an adult male that has not yet embraced his power as a man. When a woman comes to me to complain about some 'guy' she's having an issue with, I will often say, 'Your problem is the noun. You're dealing with a guy when you want to be dealing with a man.' There is a difference. Guys are afraid of their power, or don't know how to access their power, so they stay stuck in a sort of 'bro' mentality. When we're being guys, we're really good at entertaining ourselves and staying out of any serious trouble, but we're not able to take care of anyone else or really take charge of our life. When we're stuck in the immature guy mode, we stay away from anything 'serious.' We're always joking around and unable to take anything seriously. The video game industry is built around guys. The young, goofy male characters you see on TV are good examples of guys.

Too often men will hold onto their immature guy behaviors way into their middle age. Homer Simpson is a middle-aged guy — one of the many 'doofus dads' on TV. If it wasn't for their sensible women, the doofus dads would eat themselves to death or burn their houses down. The world of popular 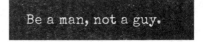 media propagates this idea, but it doesn't come from nowhere. I've heard from so many women clients over the years that their husbands and boyfriends need to grow up. When we allow ourselves to be stuck in our immaturity, we make our women into our bosses, into our mothers. It's a drag for them and a recipe for unhappiness. Be a man, not a guy.

Antidotes to Immaturity
The cure for this immature mode of being lies in the fatherly energy of the King. What do you need to take care of in your world? The immature guy can't care for or protect anyone or anything. Take stock of your life and your world. What is depending on your strength, your backbone? It's not about being more serious or mature exactly. It's about being a man instead of a boy or a guy. A man takes care of shit. What do you need to take care of?

COWARDICE

Cowardice is another very common enemy that most of us modern men fall victim to when we drift onto the Black Road. A man's bravery and fearlessness used to be measured by his willingness to face mortal and physical danger. These days, our civil society has eliminated most physical dangers of day-to-day life. Today's cowards aren't running away from combat or avoiding physical confrontations, they are hiding from life challenges. Today's cowards are running from hard truths, commitment, risk, and brutal honesty.

In the Warrior chapter we talked about not being a pussy. It's usually not that a man is actually a coward – just that cowardice as a quality – as an inner enemy – can creep into our way of being if we lose sight of our Red Road.

Cowardice takes over when we allow our fear to dictate our actions – or lack of action. We become cowards when we avoid facing what we need to face in order to live our Truth – whether the challenges are outside in our life, or inside in our hearts and minds. When we succumb to cowardice, we give up our sense of honor and self-respect. Cowardice keeps us from standing up for what we believe in.

When we're living in cowardice we become small and sneaky. We don't want other men to know we're acting cowardly. There's a reason for this. We are hard-wired as men to distrust men who show cowardice. In ancient times, when we lived in close-knit communities, men depended on each other's honor and bravery. If a man displays cowardice, we don't trust that he will have our back when the time comes. A coward will betray other people for the sake of his own safety or to gain a minor payoff. A coward will cave in and compromise his friends in order to save himself. The thing is, this quality is so pervasive in men nowadays that many men have no idea what it means to have another's back or trust other men. After reading this, you might be the first non-cowardly man in your life.

The Red Road is no place for cowardice. If we are to have backbone and walk the Red Road, we must be willing to leave our comfort zone and confront all of our inner enemies. We have to embrace risk and be willing to enter the fray, get into 'the shit' and duke it out with life to realize our vision. We need to rise and be trustworthy and brave. Our world needs brave men.

Antidotes to Cowardice

The exercises and questions I raise in the Warrior chapter will help a lot with cowardice. You'll get a huge sense of relief when you simply realize what you're being cowardly about and take some action. Take some risk. Even if you have to fail and learn from trial and error, you'll be better as a result. Cowardice is a habit of behavior, not an innate quality. Ultimately the cure for cowardice is action in the face of fear. Remember, fear doesn't always feel like fear. It can take the form of avoidance, or squirming, or rejection. Be brave. Look at how you're not brave and take action.

CALLOUSNESS

Callousness is the quality of being unconsciously hard, tough, insensitive, and sometimes even mean and brutal. Think of a hand that has callouses from hard work, and then imagine your inner being having that same kind of thickness. I'm not talking about inner strength, grit, fearlessness, or other useful kinds of firmness. I'm talking about a kind of deadness, like the dead skin on your feet and hands.

When we give in to callousness, we become what I call 'hard men.' This is when we're acting like tough guys. We avoid wholeness by denying anything in ourselves that seems too soft, or too feminine, or too vulnerable, or too weird.

Some men grow into adulthood frozen into the hard-man mold. They are the grown-up versions of the bullies and jocks who beat up gay kids in high school. They're the macho men who think they're too manly to admit any weakness. They're hard, rigid. They don't know how to relate to women, or access their own emotions. Sometimes they're mean, even brutal, and they'll tell you this is how a man is supposed to be. A hard man embraces being masculine, but he is boxed in by his limited concepts of manhood: men don't cry, men don't eat salad, men don't dance in public, etc. Often these men will also be inflexible with their opinions and prejudices. Bigots are stuck in hardness.

There are healthy qualities of toughness and grit that help us get stuff done and stand up for ourselves. But callousness is when we get stuck as the hard man. It's like a knight stuck in his suit of armor. He put it on once for a battle and now he lives with it on. He showers with it, tries to make love to his wife with it on. He tries to hug his kids, but it doesn't quite work.

When this is our default way of being, we have a hard time listening, or being compassionate, or being gentle when we need to be. Tough guys can be downright brutal and stupid, and destroy gentle things with their insensitivity. When we're stuck in our hardness, we miss

> Hard men don't age well, and don't age happily.

out on the soft side of life. When we father from a calloused place, we're unforgiving, critical, and shaming to our kids. Of course we need to be strong and firm with our kids, but kids are soft and need us to have our soft side intact to love them right. Hard men don't age well, and don't age happily.

In the American biker community – of which I am a part – there is a common acronym: DILLIGAF. You see it on t-shirts, and motorcycle helmets, even tattoos. It stands for 'Do I Look Like I Give A Fuck?' This is the creed of the hard man. Their gates are closed. They don't give a fuck. Other bikers sport the letters FTW – Fuck the World. Either of these could be battle cries for a life of fiery non-conformity: 'I don't care what you think – I'm going to live my truth and fuck the world if it doesn't understand!' But in my experience, when these acronyms are worn by men who are afflicted with Black Road callousness, they are the opposite. They are worn proudly as symbols of owner's stuckness and deep unhappiness.

Life has so many textures and nuances. A calloused hand can only feel so much. Being stuck in the hard mode is just another form of passivity. The hard man might raise his voice and push people around, but he is still paralyzed when it comes to creating a vision and crafting a conscious life. To walk the Red Road and be truly whole, we need to be able to be strong when we need to be, and tender when tenderness is called for. We fight when it's time to fight, dance when it's time to dance, and enjoy when it's time to enjoy. When we're calloused and stiff, we're stuck in one mode.

Antidotes to Callousness
The work that you do to get the Lover will act like heat to unfreeze
a great deal of your callousness. Like any other new way of being,
you have to wade into it bit by bit and allow for the transformation
to take effect. Also, really pay attention as to whether you're giving
a fuck or not. Give a fuck. Take care. Slow down. Pay attention.
This may be counter-intuitive, but the other great remedy for the
hard man is the Warrior. When your Warrior is strong you can more
easily soften and be vulnerable. If you know how to wield your
sword well, you need less armor.

DISTRACTION

The one inner enemy that almost all modern men face to some
extent is distraction. Distraction ranges from wasting time on the
internet to full-blown addiction issues. To be distracted means
to be pulled in different directions. A man with backbone on the
Red Road is a man with a vision and a purpose. When we're letting
ourselves get distracted, or indulging in habitual distractions, we're
allowing ourselves to be pulled away from our purpose and vision.
We're going off-track.

Lots of men today are very distracted by technology, always
checking our smart phones, staring at our lap-tops, listening to
headphones, watching TV, and so on. When we do this too much,
we start to live vicariously
through these virtual worlds
and aren't available to take
deep care of our real world
right in front of us. Distracted
men are like ostriches with
their heads stuck in the sand.

We go into the
distracted absent-
guy thing when
we're not turned on
by our life.

We stick our heads in the news, or in sports, or in porn. Many men today live this way. The really zoned-out distracted guys are the addicts among us. They're high, they're drunk, they're on pills, or obsessed with sex. They have given up their Red Road altogether. Their path in any given moment is the path that leads to their drug of choice, even if that drug is a woman's vagina.

Our distractions distract our actions, and take us from our life path, and they also just simply distract our attention. When we fall prey to distraction, we lose the ability to just be there. We can't focus on a conversation, an idea, or a deep feeling. We're all over the place.

Distraction itself is a kind of addiction. We use our distractions to distract us from our inner discomfort. They act like anesthesia. Food, TV, cocktails, weed, workaholism, busyness – these are all great ways for us to check out and stay numb. This is a problem when we are trying to find the Red Road. When we're trying to live a conscious life, we need to know what we're uncomfortable with so we can know what needs our focus.

We go into the distracted absent-guy thing when we're not turned on by our life. Our wife doesn't turn us on, so we turn to porn. Our job doesn't turn us on, so we spend our day browsing the internet. When we don't have a clear vision for life that demands our focus, we hang out on Facebook or constantly check our messages in case there is something calling for our attention. Life on the Red Road is rich and demanding. If we don't get juiced and excited by living our vision, then we find something that will substitute for that juice – even if it's Fantasy Football.

Lots of men are into 'white noise.' They need to always have some kind of TV or radio on in the background. It's like they need to use the noise to drown out some unpleasant voice within themselves. If we're honest, most of us do some kind of distracted behavior.

Let me be clear. I am not talking about recreation. Recreation is a whole other thing where we take some time out from our demanding Red Road life to blow off steam, or goof around, or indulge in some meaningless fun. This is actually important for men. The enemy I'm talking about is the habitual behavior of escaping and being absent when we need to be present. I'm talking about that part in us that is an avoider — a conflict avoider, a hardship avoider, a decision avoider, a life avoider.

When we are distracted, or addicted, or stoned, our power is diminished, our passion is dulled, and our purpose is thwarted. Knowing how to distract and numb yourself is an important skill for a life on the Black Road. The Black Road sucks. And it's painful and boring and unstimulating. If you don't have some way to take the edge off, it's just too uncomfortable. You have to be a little drunk or high or zoned out to get along with everyone else on the Black Road. If you're wide awake, stone-cold sober, full of purpose, passion, and power, it's impossible to stay on the Black Road. It you don't have distraction or anesthesia, you're forced to make your life have backbone.

Antidotes to Distraction

This might not sound very appealing, but if you can harness your Warrior energy and be brave, you can try to resist whatever your distracted behavior is and see what you're avoiding. I have to warn you, it may not be pretty. You might find that your distraction is keeping you from seeing or feeling some serious bullshit. But if you're to really get that Third Key, you need to get free from that very bullshit sooner or later. Sometimes our distraction behaviors are just habits that need quitting. Then it's just a matter of sucking it up and getting over the initial discomfort. Try using discipline to limit your computer time, or cut back on your alcohol/weed/TV consumption and see how you feel. Lean into your life. See what you're avoiding. If you see that things are off, fix them. That's what men do.

ANGER

Anger is the universal negative expression for men, partly because it's one of the only emotions that men are 'allowed' to have. Because of this, more complex emotions like frustration, sadness, hurt feelings, fear, determination, grief, disappointment, and many other feelings come out as some form of anger in men. Anger in and of itself isn't really a problem or inner enemy, but it's important for us to keep tabs on our anger. We need to know how to handle anger and express it well without causing destruction or poisoning ourselves or the environments where we live.

Anger is an energy that expresses itself in a wide variety of ways: pouting, cold silence, passive aggression, sarcasm, bitterness, yelling, condescending speech, tantrums, rageful driving, breaking things, punching walls, self-destructive behavior, physical violence, grumpyness. Aside from the dangerous violent expressions of anger, almost any form of expression is probably better than holding our anger in and letting it stew. When we stuff our anger down or deny our anger, it either builds up and eventually explodes, or it turns into a kind of slow rotting poison that colors our whole experience of life. We age into grumpy old men.

It's worth mentioning grumpiness. Grumpiness is a malady that many men walk around with. It's like a vague discontent that makes us irritable and generally unpleasant to be around. Because it's not explosive like rage it doesn't get us into the same kind of trouble. But it's ugly. It dims our vision and sucks the emotional air out of any space we're in.

Too many men keep more-or-less constant company with some form of anger. It's like an old rusty nail we carry around in our mouth. And when we're living in anger, we are not just poisoning ourselves, we're poisoning the environment around us as well. Many of the other inner enemies spring from anger. When we're angry we become passive, or bitter. We become hard or cruel. And let's face it – life's no fun when we're walking around angry all the time.

Whenever there is anger, there is always a frustrated desire. Always. Either there is something that we want that we can't have, or something that we don't want that we can't avoid. Whenever we find ourselves angry, we can simply check out what desires are being frustrated or what unpleasantness is being persistent. Anger is actually a good alarm bell for us that we have left the Red Road.

Antidotes to Anger

Notice when you're angry – and again remember that it might not be a typical, frowning, rageful anger. It might just be a bitter feeling, or a slight resentment. We might catch ourselves being sarcastic or putting someone down. Whatever the mode of expression, notice your anger and start investigating: What are you missing? What desire of yours is being thwarted? Then you have three simple options: You can either satisfy the desire (or eliminate the aversion), renounce the desire (let it go), or ... keep being angry.

A great remedy for grumpiness is gratitude. If you find yourself in a grumpy mood, or realize that you're a grumpy man in general, take a moment to consider what you're grateful for. Grumpy with the kids? Be grateful for the kids. Grumpy with your work? Be thankful you have a job. Often you don't need much more than this simple attitude adjustment. If it is something deeper, see the anger remedies above. You deserve to live free from anger.

SELF-EMASCULATION

Not every man will relate to this, but there is a certain kind of man today that disowns his manhood. There are some men who, for different reasons, have a sort of aversion to masculine energy and so they opt out of it. Sometimes a little bit, sometimes completely. You see a deep self-emasculation in the spiritual scenes. You see the guys who seem to want to be angels instead of men. They're the ones who offer long, breathy hugs at the end of the meditation workshop. They are the non-threatening, sweet guys who women confide in. I see this quality also among uber-intellectual types, sometimes among the hipsters. Being masculine isn't seen as being evolved or cool.

Sometimes there is almost a misandry among men. Misandry is a fancy word for man-hating. Some self-emasculated men are downright hostile toward other men or masculine energy. At the very least, self-emasculated men tend to avoid relationships with men and choose instead to surround themselves with women. They roll their eyes at athletes and look down on men who are overtly macho; they pride themselves on being allowed into the confidential inner circles of women. I call these men omega males. There is the alpha male – the strong, uber-macho, leader guy who always has to be the toughest, the strongest, the first to the finish. And there is the beta male, the lower-ranked guy that follows the alpha, and who would be an alpha if he could be. And then there is the omega male. The omega male is the guy who opts out of his manhood completely. Spiritual guys are good at this.

It's not to say that it's always a sign of disempowerment if a man is not particularly masculine. There are all kinds of strong men and some of them can be downright effeminate. In the case of spiritual men, of course there's nothing wrong with men being overtly spiritual, or sensitive, or non-threatening. The problem is when these 'noble' qualities are masking some deeper incompleteness. The problem is when we become gentle or effeminate at the expense of our authentic power and disown the loud, deep, manly parts of ourselves.

What I'm talking about is when our disowning of our masculinity springs from self-hatred or unresolved Mental Bullshit. We can't be whole if we live in a one-dimensional way. We can't focus on the

> We can't sterilize or spiritualize the blood and guts and shadow that are part of a holistic life.

positive and totally negate the hardship, the grind and grit of being an adult man. We can't sterilize or spiritualize the blood and guts and shadow that are part of a holistic life.

This inner enemy for us is a subtle one. It's not easy to admit that we somehow disown our masculinity, but many of us do. Sometimes there's a lot of work to do in this area. Sometimes there's just a hint of it. Check it out in yourself. Do you feel comfortable around other men? Do you have an aversion to masculine energy or men?

Antidotes to Self-Emasculation
The best way to combat this inner enemy is to put yourself in the presence of other men. Often times, self-emasculators avoid men — especially masculine men. If you have some of this enemy in your mix, seek out the company of men that scare you a little bit. I had to do this and still do. Because I am such a sincerely spiritual man, I want to make sure that my feet stay on the ground, so I make sure that I spend time with men who will take me down a notch if I get too spiritually goofy. It's also helped me

a great deal to have a family. There is a lot of blood and guts and gravitas when you're a father.

WHAT ABOUT YOU?

If we're honest, each of us has a combo of these Black Road inner enemies – and others too – within us. Every man has his stronger moments and his weaker, stupid ones. There's no blame here and no shame. It's all about awareness. This work is about recognizing what we're unconsciously doing, and choosing consciously what we want to do and how we want to be. These inner enemies aren't listed here to separate us from each other, or to help us to evaluate or judge other men. These aren't labels to put on ourselves or others: 'Ah-ha! That guy is totally a passive, immature man!' There's a distracted man, a coward, and an immature guy in each of us – and there is a deep and steady big man too. We just have to choose which road we want to walk, which of these qualities we want to invest in and feed.

Assuming you have your good days and your bad days, which way do you tend to go when you move away from your Red Road? Do you get floppy and distracted, or do you revert into hardness and machismo? Do you become a hybrid, like a hard, immature guy or a naive coward? Let yourself off the hook a little bit, and realize that we're all learning. No one really showed us the ropes on how to be powerful men, so we had to wing it. Chances are, we didn't wing it perfectly. This examination can be fun – even funny. On the path to deep happiness and True Power, one of the greatest skills you can have is the ability to laugh at yourself, especially at the antics of your mind and ego. This whole thing is a process of trial and error. It's good to give yourself space to learn in this way.

BRUTAL HONESTY
Make a list of your top inner enemies and describe
the way they could sabotage your purpose and
vision. Come up with a plan of attack to combat
each one with the antidotes I've suggested above.

SUMMING IT UP

Inner Enemies – unconscious qualities of being that take us off
the Red Road.

Passivity – the passive part of us that lies down when we are
challenged. The antidote lies in the First Key – knowing our
purpose and choosing every moment of our life.

Immaturity – too many of us are not really men, we're guys – man-
aged boys. We rise out of our immaturity by caring for and serving
our world.

Cowardice – when our fear dictates our actions we become small
and sneaky. Take risk. Take action, break the habit of avoidance.

Callousness – tough guys are stuck in their armor. The antidote for
hardness is the Lover.

Distraction – this keeps us out of the real world and not facing our
responsibilities. See what you're distracting yourself from and take
action to make your self and your life the way you choose.

Anger – this is caused by frustrated desire and poisons us and our
world. See what you're frustrated about and either fix it or let go
of your desires.

Self-Emasculation – some men outright avoid their deep
masculine power. Spend time around men who can help you find
your balls and get your feet on the ground.

13

BROTHERHOOD

Do you have good men in your life? This is a question I ask every man who comes into my practice. The answer is usually no. When people ask me, 'What is *one thing* you recommend to men who want to find their backbone?' I always say, 'Get more good men in your life.'

If you really want to have a good, solid, masculine backbone, you need to have some brothers. Brothers are different from just buddies or pals. Brothers are men that you count on and who count on you. Brothers are men that you feel genuine love and devotion for. You'll sacrifice for a brother. You'll take a bullet for a brother.

Your men are your team, and every man needs a team. Your men will be there for you to pull you up when you're down, and applaud you when you're doing great, and bust your balls if you get too arrogant. But to have this kind of great support – you need good men in your life. Remember the Three Keys: your brothers will help you stay on track with living your vision, and they'll help you stay clear of your bullshit.

Most men these days are cut off from other men. Most men today lack almost any male friends, let alone 'brothers.' In the old days there were barber shops, and bowling leagues, and male-dominated work environments where men could be men in an unapologetic way. Now it's not like that. Most work environments are mixed gender, and the old-school male environments are at risk of extinction.

For me, I found that, as I got older, I had fewer and fewer close man friends. Sometimes I would be in mixed-gender social situations with my female partner's friends' men. But rarely did I spend any quality time with men alone. I preferred to be around women, not just because I am heterosexual and find them attractive, but for their friendship. I was much more comfortable with women than with men. Before I worked out my own shit with my dad, with my own manhood, and with masculine energy in general, I would keep my distance from other men – especially very masculine men. It wasn't conscious: it just worked out that way. As I went into my own journey with this stuff, I had to sort out this part. I had to learn how to give and receive man love.

MAN LOVE

Yes. I said it. Man love. There is a way that we love each other that is different from the way we love anyone else. Man love is something that develops best in the absence of women. For most of us, our love will tend to flow along the path of least resistance. And for most of us, that means toward the women in our life. This is nothing against women. It's just that something happens when men are only with other men.

This man love thing is important to work out for many reasons. The main one is that we need other men in our corner to help us

> Being around men – especially masculine men – helps us to toughen up.

to be in our bigness. We can't do all this alone and it's really not the role of the women in our life to help us to learn how to be better men. The other reason is simply that the more we learn how to love and be loved by other men, the easier it is for us to love our own masculine self.

Something entirely different happens for men when they are together and only around other men – something really cool. There is something in us that relaxes. At first, if a man is not used to it, it can be downright uncomfortable.

If we're not at peace with our own masculine power, we might really avoid male-only situations. This was definitely the case for me. I never played sports or served in the military. The closest thing I ever had to male camaraderie came from playing in garage bands in high school and college. But females and female attention were always in the mix in the rock-and-roll culture. As I embarked on the path toward having backbone, I had to learn how to be around men. It was hard at first. I remember taking a precision motorcycling course taught by retired motorcycle cops and almost crying when they yelled at me for making a mistake. Being around men – especially masculine men – helps us to toughen up.

Man-to-Man Intimacy

Most men today don't know how to make new man friends, or nurture new friendships, or share intimacy with other men. I know there's a gay joke waiting to be said here. The word intimacy these days is often just a euphemism for sex. But it doesn't mean sex. Intimacy in this case means a deeper connection.

Most men, especially by the time they reach middle age, have only a few male friends and often these friendships aren't really close. Some men may happen to have held on to a few friends from their youth or from college. Other men might have a few buddies from work, or male siblings or uncles who provide male support. But for the vast majority of men, this is an area that we need to develop.

What I'm talking about here are relationships with men where you have each other's backs. I am speaking of friendships where you trust each other with your secrets and go to each other for support.

YOU NEED A MALE CONFIDANT

It's pretty common for men to get all of their intimate needs met by their romantic partner. This is especially true for married men or men in committed relationships. Our wives and girlfriends become our confidantes. We share our heart, our hopes and dreams and fears with them and then present a cool superficial exterior to the men in our lives. I suggest that we almost want to have the opposite.

Why Men vs Women

It's important to have people who we can speak with, who we can be totally open and honest with, who won't judge us, and who will keep our secrets. It's just that the best candidate for this is almost never our wife or girlfriend. Please understand something: our women don't want to hear about our weaknesses. They don't want to hear about our fears or our insecurities. They will listen. They will lick our wounds and hold us and let us cry. In the beginning they might even like it. It might make them feel like they are with a 'safe' guy. But over time, it bites us in the ass.

Our women lose respect and sexual attraction to us when we share all of our weaknesses and fears with them. Deep down, we are all wired like cavepeople. On the socialized, intellectual level a woman might want a man who is open about everything. Some insecure women might even insist that we have no secrets. But deep down, the cavewoman inside her doesn't want a weak caveman. Women want men who have their shit together. They want men who can be protectors – warriors, not neurotic worriers. It's not that we have to hide all of our feelings and be closed off to our women, but if we learn to spare them a ringside view of our most unenlightened moments, we'll be doing them, and our relationship, and ourselves a big favor.

LEARNING TO SHUT THE FUCK UP

Our grandfathers' generation of men were largely in denial of their inner life. They were mostly about self-denial, sacrifice, and adherence to duty. Maybe they didn't even know what their feelings were, or what their doubts were. And if they did have them, they largely kept them totally to themselves. They were stoic to a fault.

In our post-1960s generation, we men have mostly adopted the opposite way. We are uber-indulgent about our feelings. We feel we need to examine and honor every doubt, every feeling, every discomfort, and then talk about it – especially with the women in our lives. We are best friends with our women and share 'everything.' We feel the need to share every insecurity, every worry, every idea. We jump into gossipy conversations with them and become their confidants. This is mostly a bad idea for many reasons. For one thing, it kills the passion in our relationships, it takes away our women's ability to trust us. We do the over-sharing in some strange attempt to gain their trust, but it does the opposite. Deep down, they want to know that we are stable and have our emotional shit together. It doesn't help anything when we become open books for them to read. We think we need to be ready to cry with them, or let ourselves be small and weak and let them hold us and be our strength, but it's a bad habit.

Privacy is a good thing. We should shut the door when we use the toilet and we should also spare them the gory details of our emotional turmoil. We don't have to pretend that we don't have emotional weakness or inner turmoil – it's just that we don't need to spray it all over them. We can have boundaries. We can learn to shut up when we are with our women, and then share our weakness with men. There is something to be said for learning to hold some things and not blab everything that comes into our head.

Haragei

In Japanese, they have a word: *haragei* – literally it means 'stomach art.' It is the art of being able to 'stomach' something. This is what the Japanese corporate samurai use to win business negotiations. They shut the fuck up, and wait, and use their words very judiciously. Instead of showing all their cards, they let their opponent show their weaknesses. I think there's a lot we can learn as modern men from the masters of haragei.

When it comes to our inner life and our feelings, I am definitely not talking about denial. That was our grandfathers' road. No. On the Red Road we know ourselves – we honor what we're feeling and learning, and desiring or fearing fully. We just have a place in us to hold it. We hold it, we handle it. It's not all over the place.

It's not about keeping everything secret. It is important to speak our truth and share our concerns or dreams. It is important to say things out loud and get reality checked from time to time.

It is important to vent our feelings and share our heart's truth and cry if we need to. But can we learn to share this stuff with other men? If we do, we get a totally different kind of feedback. Men will hear us out, maybe offer some feedback or support and send us on our way. We can get messy and hash shit out with our men, and then go home more integrated. We can share our weakness with our men and then be able to go home and be the strong pillar that our relationships and families need. Not in a fake denial-based way, but in a true way.

We need to learn to not do all of our 'processing' in our romantic relationships – and definitely not with our family, our kids. Imagine dad sitting at the dinner table: 'Kids, wife, I just want to share something. You're my beloved family and I don't want to keep any secrets from you. So I want to share with you that I'm really afraid my business is going to fail, and sometimes I think about killing myself. And, oh yeah, I worry that I'm not strong enough to be a good father. I just wanted to be honest and let you know.'

Can you imagine? If we were to say the same things in a men's group, the reaction would be completely different. Chances are, there would probably be a bunch of men who would say, 'Yep – me too!' Hopefully there will be some older men who will be able to share their wisdom and experience of passing through these kinds of patches and coming out of them alright. The younger men in the group will gain the benefit of hearing the men hash out these little inner demon voices with fearlessness and steadiness. We get it off our chest, get some reality check from the group, and get to hear ourselves think out loud for a minute. No harm done, and probably there will be some good healing. Then we go home, shut the fuck up, and take care of whatever we have signed on to do in our lives. It's a great thing.

Haragei is also important when it comes to having our brothers' backs. It's super important that we learn how to hold in confidence the things that other men tell us and that we are men who can hear potent stuff from other men – and then practice haragei and shut the fuck up about it. If we go home from our men's group

> You need to have a man or men in your life that you can share all of that with, and more.

and say, 'Honey, guess what! David shared tonight that he wants to kill himself!' What's that going to do? If that comes back around to David's wife, or David's students, what then? Or if we get in a fight with our woman and feel backed into a corner and start blabbing, 'In his book David said we shouldn't really talk to our women! He said that we should just shut the fuck up because *you* can't handle hearing about *my feelings*!' We need to learn to hold our tongue.

Please don't share everything from this book with the woman in your life. Take it in, practice it, prove me right or prove me wrong. Then share some of it – *if you must* for some reason. Haragei is an art worth learning.

Confidential

The point of having a confidant is to have a safe place where you can say anything without it causing trouble. If our confidant is our intimate partner, we won't share anything controversial about them or anything controversial about us that might affect them. It kind of defeats the whole purpose. Think about it: if you have issues in the relationship – especially doubts or desires for other women or other unsavory issues – you're not going to share those. You need to have a man or men in your life that you can share all of that with, and more.

There's a saying, 'We're only as sick as our secrets.' It's important to have a place where we can say anything and share even our darkest thoughts, fears, desires, and situations so that they don't take root in our 'inner land' and turn into troublesome life situations.

I remember an especially good night at a men's group when one of the younger men asked for advice. He was in a committed relationship with a nice girl and was basically happy, but he was having a lot of desire for other women. He worked with a lot of beautiful young women and was constantly lusting after them. He hadn't told anyone about his situation and was worried that his wandering eye was going to harm his relationship. He wondered if he needed to tell his girlfriend, or what it 'meant' about their status. Luckily for him, we had a good collection of men, mostly older than him, who were able to laugh at his 'problem' and put him at ease about it. Just getting it off his chest would have probably been enough. But he also got the benefit of the masculine life wisdom in the group. We had all been there and still go there. We were all in the same boat and could share our experience, strength, and insight with him in that masculine context.

Had he shared his feelings with his girlfriend, it would have most likely just freaked her out and caused him to try to stuff his feelings down. Because he said it all out loud, he got to know that he was totally normal and that the feelings didn't actually mean anything about his relationship with his girlfriend. He also got some real-life, no-judgment advice about the risks and consequences of acting on his feelings.

The lusty young man thought he was all alone. He was so relieved to know he wasn't. I've seen that same thing happen with money issues, tax problems, business fears, shame about childhood molestation, and a whole host of other issues where men were brave enough to voice something they thought was their private cross to bear, only to learn that other men had the same issue or had overcome the same obstacle.

Your Men

It's important to say here that we mustn't be naive. Just because someone is male doesn't mean he is one of 'your men.' Many married men are surrounded by the husbands of their wife's friends. Unless there are special circumstances, these men are not the ones you want in your confidential circle. Why? Because, chances are, your wife's friends' husbands haven't yet done this work and don't yet understand the solemn duty to keep our man conversations confidential. They will go blab your issues to their wife-confidantes and then the whole thing is out of the bag. It's important to choose wisely, and even have explicit conversations about confidence. Don't assume that any modern man has honor. Unfortunately, these days, most don't. The whole idea of holding things in confidence has to be agreed on and practiced and learned.

In our NYC men's group, we have a zero-tolerance confidentiality clause that we read at the beginning of each meeting. Men

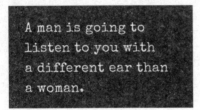

A man is going to listen to you with a different ear than a woman.

in the group have to promise to keep everything said in the group 100 per cent confidential. Men who violate this are removed instantly. It sucks, believe me: we've had to ask a man not to come back to the group after he shared sensitive info with his wife, who then shared it with the wife of another group member, which caused that man to get into some real shitty conversations.

The man or men that you choose to be in your circle need to be clear about this. And you have to make it explicit: 'You can't say any of this to anyone, including your wife. Got it?' The 'including your wife' part is important. Eventually, you get into this habit of keeping other men's personal stuff to yourself.

THE MASCULINE EAR

Your man friends also play the very simple and important role of providing the masculine perspective in your life. If you share your trials and tribulations with women, you'll get one kind of support – a female perspective. With men, it will be a little different.

Chances are, your man friends will not so much want to look deeply into your eyes and listen to you – they will more likely want to be shoulder to shoulder with you. In child development, this is called 'parallel play.' If you need to have a conversation with a man or even with a boy, take him for a walk or a drive. Go fishing together and talk in the boat. Work on a project together. Grab a beer and sit on the porch watching the world pass by and talk there. To women, it might seem that we're not really connected deeply but we are.

Also, a man is going to listen to you with a different ear than a woman. For the most part, women like to talk. And they enjoy getting into drama. For the most part, men do not like to talk and are not fans of too much drama. So if you're speaking with your man friend, there is an economy to the speech. There will be fewer words; the conversation won't go on and on, round and round. We've got shit to do. And also, your man friend isn't interested in drama. He will help you to get to the bottom of whatever is happening and not add drama or extra energy to what you're speaking about. The masculine ear is always listening for the point. What's the point? What's the bottom line? How can we finish this? You can let him know if you want advice or not. Men do like to give advice. In our men's group we have a default policy of no advice. Advice is only given when it's asked for. Otherwise, we are there to listen, share our own experience, and move on. It is so refreshing.

And a man's ear is not as fragile as a woman's – especially your woman's. Remember, you woman doesn't want to hear about your worries and troubles. If you freak out to your woman, that can take you down a notch in her eyes. She might respect you or desire you less. Your man friend's ear is ready for whatever you have to say. Here's an example: A couple of years ago, I had a mole on my head that looked bad. I put off having it checked for skin cancer for more than a year. When I finally found myself in the doctor's waiting room, I was worried. I started writing a text message to my wife: 'At doctor's office, worried about this mole. Aware that it could be very bad news.'

Before I hit send, Thor (or Odin, or Shiva, or one of the other masculine gods) must have smiled on me, because I thought again. I deleted the text to her and wrote this text to my friend Ron: 'At doctor, getting scary mole checked.'

He wrote back simply, 'Yikes. Let me know what happens.'

Had I sent the text to my wife, it would have most definitely gotten me a non-desired result. Best-case scenario, she would have ignored it, or minimized my fear, or responded with some worse fear of her own. Then I may have gotten all sulky: 'She doesn't care!' Worst case, she would have been totally freaked out by my fear and gone into a panic or worry about it. Ron's simple response was all I needed. I wasn't alone, but I also didn't need to have a bunch of drama heaped onto the situation.

MAN FUN

Along with the important therapeutic value of having some close male friends to share with, it's also fun. There is something that is so valuable about being 'out with the boys.' Even if out with the boys is something like dinner with your close man friend. Sometimes, without even realizing it, we compromise with our women when it comes to what we choose to do, eat, or enjoy in our free time. There are all kinds of simplistic and dumb versions of boys' nights out: drinking, tail chasing, card games, etc. Of course there's nothing wrong with this sort of thing, but we're seeking something deeper and higher, right?

For me, I get this time in with my men motorcycling. There isn't much talking; we're mostly on the road, sharing that intense experience in a parallel way. I don't have that much in common with most of my motorcycle friends but it doesn't matter. We get outside, get our fix of danger and action, we have our solitude when we're riding, and then we have the fellowship when we stop. Sometimes we eat, sometimes we ride somewhere beautiful in nature and stop there and hang out. We talk about work, we talk about our bikes. We don't have to be gentle with each other; we don't have to worry about how we look. It's something my female partner and most of my female friends would not be into. That's just it – it's a time of non-compromise. We can cuss if we want to, we can talk about motorcycles as much as we want. For me it's motorcycles. What would it be for you?

BEING THERE

The other important thing to say here is that when you make the time to hang out with other men you are doing them a service. Even if you don't feel that you need it for your own wellbeing, you can do it for the sake of the men you're spending time with. I feel a real sense of duty toward the men in my life. Of course this goes for the men who have hired me as a teacher, but it also goes for my friends. It's important to me and it's a part of my honor that I am there for them and ready and willing to have their backs and go out of my way to support them.

LOST BROTHERS

Ever wonder what happened to old male friends? It's good to look back and remember old friends that you've had over the years. When our relationships with romantic partners end, we have to break up and negotiate the terms of the separation. When our relationships with our men end, often times, there is little or nothing said. Sometimes relationships just fizzle out, other times we have a beef with a man and decide to distance ourselves. Sometimes there is a tremendous amount of pain involved in our man break-ups. But we're good at sweeping emotionally uncomfortable things under the rug. I suggest doing a little review and really examining the major relationships you've had with men in your life, how those relationships ended, and seeing what you learn about yourself in the process.

BRUTAL HONESTY

Take some time to go back and list the main close relationships you've had with men, along with any other male relationships that ended in a painful or mysterious way. For each man on the list, write a few sentences about the good times you had, and then write about the end. Why did you part ways? What resentments are you harboring? Be brutally honest about your part in the relationships. Were you a good friend? If not, what did you do or fail to do that may have contributed to the breakup? Don't be too hard on yourself, but don't be too easy either. If you find yourself feeling some sadness or feeling of loss or grief, good. Feel it. See what actions your feelings inspire. If you get the impulse to reach out and connect with old friends, follow that impulse. It's never been easier to track people down.

MAKE AMENDS

If you have men on your list that you have wronged in some way, or if there are situations that ended poorly and have left you with a feeling of remorse, make amends. Reach out to the men that you have somehow slighted and acknowledge the pain you have caused. You might have actual financial or material amends to make too. You be the judge of how far you want to go. In AA, there is a 9th Step which suggests that we make 'direct amends to such people whenever possible, except when to do so would injure them or others.'

THE MEN'S GROUP

A men's group is a semi-formal group that meets regularly for the expressed purpose of support. What you do, where you meet, who is in your group, and what kind of support you offer is totally up to you. I will share the guidelines that I offer men when they ask my advice about setting up a group.

It's so simple. All you need is three or more men and a place to meet. I say three because only then do you have enough to have a circle. There is a power to a circle of men that is greater than simple one-on-one time. You can bullshit or manipulate one man. It's much harder to bullshit two men – even harder to bullshit a room full of men. Having more than one other person also serves to lessen some of the social awkwardness and intimacy of a face-to-face.

Then you have a set amount of time to meet. I suggest no more than 90 minutes. An hour and a half is enough. Then you need a topic or something to base the discussion around. It helps if there is someone moderating or chairing the group. Afterward, you might want to add an optional social time – food, beers, etc. Here are more details.

Chairman

It's good if the group has at least a couple of men who are the caretakers of the group. These men make sure the group keeps going and look after the logistical needs.

Our group uses a 'rotating' chairman. Each meeting has a different man take the 'chair.' The chairman decides the topic and lets the group know the topic ahead of time. We use Facebook. We have a private FB group where we post group info. Then the chairman gets there early and makes sure the room is set up. During the meeting, the chairman is responsible for keeping the flow going and keeping the time. Simple.

Who to Include?

I suggest starting with personal invitations. Get two or three other men who want to start a group and go from there. You can each invite other men, but go slow at first. In the beginning you may want to check with the other members before inviting someone new. You want men who are as gung-ho as possible when you start. Later, as the group has its own energy, you can invite more reluctant men or people that you're trying to turn onto the work. I strongly suggest having anyone who is new to the work read this book as a primer.

What to Do?

Here's the format we use in our group. It seems to be easily replicable and has great results. We do a 90-minute group every two weeks. We usually meet in my office space, which is already set up for sessions and workshops, so it's kind of perfect. It's fine to do it in a living room or any room where you can feel free to say whatever you want without others hearing you. It's best to have it in a private place rather than a bar or restaurant. The chairperson starts by setting up the chairs in a circle and lighting a candle. The chairperson then welcomes everyone and asks one of the men to read our little preamble that we use. Our preamble is a laminated sheet with the following on it:

We are here to gather and share our experience, strength, and wisdom with each other to support our common path of living as conscious, empowered men in today's world.

We are not here to give advice, complain about our problems, brag or bullshit. We are here to improve ourselves, learn, grow, and enjoy the support of other men.

Each group session will gather around a theme. This is the place where you can share whatever you need to, but, when possible, keep your sharing related to the theme and be respectful of time and the need for other members to share.

Total confidentially of everything you hear is an absolute requirement. Our agreement to hold everything said in confidence is essential to create a safe space for everyone to heal and grow and be authentic.

After the preamble, the chairman can invite new members to introduce themselves. After that he introduces the theme. The theme can be very simple. It can be general, like 'Our journey as men,' or it might be specific, like 'Our relationship to money.' If you know the people in your group well and have a strong level of rapport, you can have humorous themes like 'Slaves to poon,' or 'Learning to shut the fuck up.' The themes should be meaningful to the chairman and also relevant to others in the group. You wouldn't want to have something like 'The trials and tribulations of being a fireman' if you're the only fireman in the group. If your group were made up of firemen, this would be a great topic.

After introducing the topic, the chairperson should share his personal connection to the topic and why he chose it. The chairperson may choose to have a reading that is relevant. I wrote this whole book with the intention that it could be used in this way. Find a short passage that strikes you, read it, and share with the group what it means to you.

When the theme has been introduced, you go around the circle and give each man a chance to share his own journey as it relates to the topic. We leave it open for the first person to volunteer, and after that go clockwise around the circle. Men can always choose to 'pass' when it's their turn or ask to postpone their share until later. But the round-robin style is great because it takes off the pressure to volunteer. Everyone gets to speak and you know when your turn is coming. The chairman also gets a chance to share in the first round. This way he can speak about personal matters later that don't need to fit in with the theme.

In the first round, we don't do 'cross-talk.' Men are expected to just listen as each person speaks. We don't use a 'talking stick' – a ceremonial stick that gets passed from one speaker to another – but some groups like that sort of thing. After we get all the way around the room once, we have an open discussion until the end of the session. Advice is only given if asked for. This is important. Men love to give advice, and when they do they often miss out on the personal impact the topic has for them; they go into the advisor mode. At the very end of the session, you might want to have a short period of silent meditation. Meditation can also be done at the beginning to center the men and help them shift into group mode.

We keep our group very simple. There are no initiations or requirements for 'membership.' There are groups who do have these things but we try to keep it 'easy in – easy out.' Because we know who is there from meeting to meeting, we can trust that the men there are sincere. But different groups of men will have more or less stringent requirements for membership. The men in the group first and foremost need to feel safe and able to be open.

After our meetings we go out for tacos at a local place. The men who drink get beers. The men who don't just get tacos. Once a month we do a Sunday breakfast at a local restaurant owned by one of the group members.

Make it Count
It's a powerful thing to share your intimate material with a room full of men. The men's group isn't the time to show a front or wear a mask. It's the time to really be open and true and 'get it out there.' Remember, you're only as sick as your secrets.

Confidentiality

The importance of a confidential discussion cannot be overstated. Just as with your man friends, in your men's group the men need to be able to air whatever they need to. This includes infidelities and other things that could get them in trouble. It must be understood that members are not to share a single word that was discussed. This can even include the themes and topics introduced by the chairman. Of course, if you're telling another man about the group, you can tell him the sorts of things that are discussed. But you especially want to keep the group material private and confidential from the women in your life. Not only could it jam the other men up if their private business gets spread around, you also run the risk of getting the topic shit on. The topics discussed in men's group are for the men in the men's group. Your wife won't understand why you were discussing 'slaves to poon.' At worst she would be offended, or at least make fun of it.

Brothers vs Buddies

You don't have to be friends with everyone in your group. In fact, sometimes it's great to have men in a group that are not your social group. It can be really helpful to have outsiders' perspectives on your life. If you were just meeting with your friends or the husbands of your wife's friends, it would be a different kind of group. In our group some of us are friends, some aren't. Some men go out after for tacos, some don't. Easy in – easy out. This way it's not personal if someone comes or doesn't come. This way we aren't afraid of hurting each other's feelings if we have something pointed to say in the group. We shouldn't feel social pressure in the group. We shouldn't feel that we have to put on a show or an act in any particular way. The group is there for us. We are there for the group.

THE MAN DATE

Yep. It's exactly what it sounds like. It's a date with a man. As an adult, it can be really difficult to create that circle of men that you need to support you in your bigness. But it's totally worth doing.

Like with the men's group, the man date is much easier with a man who has read this book and gets the basic gist. I'm not going to bullshit you: it can be damn awkward. First, asking a man out on a date, then, after the date, deciding on how to take the relationship forward. But it's really the only way to do it. You can plan group events that make it a little less intimate, but it defeats the purpose a bit. The aim of the man date is to forge a new relationship with a man that can grow into a brotherhood. It is forging an alliance of sorts.

If both men have read this book, the ice is already broken. If not, then you have to decide whether you want to reveal your motive or not. You can just choose to keep it under cover and invite a man for a beer or a coffee or something and see how it goes. Or, you can just put it out there. In my experience, most men are totally on board and know exactly what you mean when you say, 'I need to make a point of spending more time with other men.' And, like with other dating scenarios, sometimes it works, and sometimes it doesn't. Sometimes you score, sometimes you only get to first base, sometimes you strike out. Best-case scenario: you go on these dates and gradually build up a base of men you can trust and who you enjoy being around.

I am immensely grateful for 'my men.' I like to shoot random text messages and emails to them. Sometimes the texts are about important stuff happening in my life, sometimes they are just jokes or stupid pictures. But we keep each other on each other's radars. We keep that man love flowing.

SUMMING IT UP

The Brother – if you really want to be a have backbone, you need to have some brothers – men who you trust and you can have a deep friendship with.

Man-to-Man Intimacy – every man needs to learn to have male confidants and men to share his secrets, weaknesses, and vulnerabilities. Learn to spare your woman from knowing every gory detail of your inner life.

Men's Groups – an important resource for any man on the Red Road.

Man Date – exactly what it sounds like. It's a 'date' with a man (preferably one who has read this book). It's the only way to make new male friends and build your group of brothers.

PRACTICAL SUGGESTION

Take action. Take stock of the men in your life and consider how you can up the level of man love in your life. Share this book with someone. Organize a man date. Find a men's group. Make it your goal to spend more quality time with men.

14

NINE ESSENTIAL PRACTICES

Here are the top nine things you can do *now* to fortify your backbone and start cultivating purpose, passion, and power.

1. GET MORE GOOD MEN AROUND YOU

See Chapter 13 on being a brother. This can't be overstated. Join a men's group or create one.

2. GET OUT INTO THE WILDERNESS

Get outdoors. Get connected to nature. There are so many good things that happen when a man goes into the wild.

For one thing, we don't have to hold back our power when we're in the wilderness. No matter how strong we are, we're not going to break the forest. No matter how big we get, we're not going to intimidate or disempower the ocean. In fact, the wilderness's bigness demands us to be bigger. It brings out our masculine power. We have to use our senses when we're in the wild. We need grit to persevere on a mountain hike or to camp out when it's cold. When you're in the wilderness, you can't be half awake. It demands that you are alert.

The wilderness is your man-temple. It doesn't matter what it is. The forest, the ocean, the desert ... anywhere where it's untamed. If you can find some 'dangerous' wilderness, even better. Of course, you want to be smart and not overestimate your skills. Don't go climbing mountains or jumping into big ocean surf unless you know what you're doing. If you don't know what you're doing – get some training. Take a basic survival course; learn simple outdoor skills like building fires or putting up shelters.

Spending time in the wilderness helps us to know what's essential and what's extra. It helps us appreciate the simple things and clear ourselves out. I lead retreats in the wilderness every year. We spend time around the fire, walking in silence, and getting deep doses of the wild medicine that nature provides.

3. FIND A MAN HOBBY

Find an activity you do with other men or that connects you to the power you most need to enhance. If you need to enhance your Mystic, take up Tai Chi or meditation. If your Warrior needs some help, take archery lessons or learn to do something dangerous. Bring your Lover to a music class or dancing lessons. Figure it out for yourself, but let it be something that gets you into the company of other men.

4. STUDY MEN

Find men you admire and study them. Read their biographies, learn about men from history. Interview old men in your life. In general, start to notice the men in your life and see what you can learn from them. You might learn how to be. You might learn how not to be. Go out of your way to connect to men at parties and mixed social situations. Talk to them, learn about their life and speak to them about the stuff you're learning here. You'll be amazed at what you learn.

5. GET YOUR BODY RIGHT

Take a deep inventory of your physical health and fitness. Go to the doctor and get your heart, prostate, and colon checked. Learn about men's health issues and get on top of anything you may have brewing. Get your diet in shape. Stop eating processed foods and drinking massive sugary sodas. Get your testosterone level checked. Low 'T' makes you passive, fat, and depressed. There is an epidemic of low 'T' levels in modern men. Get the actual number. Your doctor will only tell you normal or abnormal, but the normal range is 250–1100. That's a huge range. Below 250 they want to give you treatments. Above 1100, I don't know – maybe they hire you out to the circus. Whatever. Get yours checked and if it's low, learn about the hormone and how you can naturally boost yours to a good strong level. Be fearless and assess your fitness level and, if need be, get a trainer and get your ass in shape. You have a lot of living to do, and to do it, you will need a good, strong, healthy body.

6. DO HARD THINGS

Make friends with challenge. Start consciously doing hard things for the sake of making yourself stronger. Take the stairs instead of the elevator. Have honest conversations, even if you're scared shitless. Take risks, live your vision. Whatever doesn't kill you makes you stronger.

7. GET TRAINING

Assess the areas that you are weak in and get the training you need to be strong. Find a mentor or mentors who can help you learn and grow your backbone in whatever way you need to.

8. DO THE BACKBONE EXERCISES

If you have read through to this point and didn't do the exercises along the way, go back through and do them faithfully, rigorously. They will provide a good inventory of your current state and help you break through to the next level of purpose, passion, and power. When you've completed all the exercises, find a good man to share your findings with. It's massively powerful to hear yourself say all that aloud and get the support and input from a trusted brother.

9. DO SOMETHING

Do anything. But don't do nothing. This is your life, brother! Your time, your days, your weeks, your months, your years are precious.

You can choose to do amazing things and get the most of your time, or you can wait. It's really up to you.

I believe with all my heart and soul that you deserve the best of life, and life deserves the best of you. As men, we have a massive job ahead of us. We have missions to accomplish, families to take care of, purposes to fulfill. Do this deep work, this backbone work and know yourself inside and out and make yourself the most excellent man you can be. And then live the hell out of life for as many days as you're given. Leave nothing on the table. Remember this passage from Tecumseh's Creed:

> *When it comes your time to die, be not like those whose hearts are filled with the fear of death, so that when their time comes they weep and pray for a little more time to live their lives over again in a different way. Sing your death song and die like a hero going home.*

I hope this book has been a stepping stone for you on your Red Road. Congratulations for taking the time to invest in yourself in this way. It's my hope that you pass this on to other men and that you come back to these pages again and again. Also, keep in touch! Come see us for a weekend or workshop and let me know if there is anything I can do to support you walking your path. Until then, I wish you purpose, passion, and power in your life.

Live Hard, Live True

WATKINS

Sharing Wisdom Since
1893

The story of Watkins Publishing dates back to March 1893, when John M. Watkins, a scholar of esotericism, overheard his friend and teacher Madame Blavatsky lamenting the fact that there was nowhere in London to buy books on mysticism, occultism or metaphysics. At that moment Watkins was born, soon to become the home of many of the leading lights of spiritual literature, including Carl Jung, Rudolf Steiner, Alice Bailey and Chögyam Trungpa.

Today our passion for vigorous questioning is still resolute. With over 350 titles on our list, Watkins Publishing reflects the development of spiritual thinking and new science over the past 120 years. We remain at the cutting edge, committed to publishing books that change lives.

DISCOVER MORE ...

Read our blog

Watch and listen to
our authors in action

Sign up to
our mailing list

JOIN IN THE CONVERSATION

 WatkinsPublishing   @watkinswisdom

▶ WatkinsPublishingLtd   8+ +watkinspublishing1893

Our books celebrate conscious, passionate, wise and happy living.
Be part of the community by visiting

www.watkinspublishing.com